'I remember as a young Christia[n] overhearing a conversation abou[t the role of women in church] thought to myself, "That's not my problem." I could not have been more wrong. By the grace of God, I was led to repentance. I have gone on to have the privilege of working alongside Nay and other women. They exceed me in character and contribution to God's kingdom, without whom we'd all be impoverished. The triune God has made men and women to display together his beautiful goodness in his world. And it should matter to all of us how we interact and serve alongside one another. I've found Nay's work in *She Needs* to be a helpful window into the painful experience of women of which I might otherwise have been ignorant. I lament my own failures and those that have been knowingly or unknowingly built into much of what we do. I'm challenged by the honest experience of women in the Church and inspired to do all I can to see, hear and honour women better.'
Dave Bish, Associate Minister, Beeston Free Evangelical Church

'As a girl, I felt I was able to do nearly anything I would like to achieve, regardless of my gender. As a woman, though, I have often felt inadequate and not enough. Because that is when I heard for the first time: Christian women should not do such and such. Really? It sounds like Nay's story, but it is mine. But Nay has not stayed within that framing; she is writing in *She Needs* about how God has spoken to her not to give in to circumstances but to expand the frame and invite men and women alike to step in and step up. To be defined by God's calling and going ahead fixing the leaky pipe, even when it costs her so much to do so. In confidence and vulnerability.

'This book is an invitation to join this exciting and life-changing journey and meet the needs of women around the globe, so as to build God's kingdom together. We are better together!'
Evi Rodemann, Cheerleader for the next generation, LeadNow e.V., Lausanne

'I felt frustrated as the words fell out of my mouth for the umpteenth time, "We don't invite women speakers because we don't know many good female Bible handlers." I wasn't frustrated with the student who had asked the question, but with the culture of which I was a part and which I helped to perpetuate, which meant that gifted and godly women weren't given the opportunity to develop or deploy their God-given abilities. For the men, it was almost expected that they would have a go at leading Bible studies and speaking, and those with natural ability would be put through a pre-prepared conveyor belt of opportunities. But for the women, there was no such well-trodden path. Well, unless they left for another country or theological camp. No wonder we didn't know many good female handlers – what we meant by that was women who had gone through a privileged system of training. But this isn't how it is meant to be. Everyone who is called by God should be invested in to serve in the appropriate context for their calling. And so, the stories of women overlooked and under-trained need to be told. We must see and feel the struggle, so that those who are the gate keepers to opportunity might fling the gates open. I trust this book will do just that.'
Jonathan Thomas, Pastor

'Nay Dawson articulates the subtle sexism so many of us have experienced in the Church. Her understanding and compassion are evident on every page of this book, along with ideas for ways forward for all of us, as we seek to serve Jesus wholeheartedly with our co-workers in Christ.'
The Revd Jo Trickey, Church Advocate, London Institute for Contemporary Christianity

'Nay is addressing many of the issues women face in ministry, but she is also encouraging and helping us to start the conversation that will help us to make the necessary changes. To be honest I got a bit emotional reading through this book because I recognized so many of the hard and painful stories and experiences from my own life in church and ministry. But I also felt encouraged to see myself as a woman being called to contribute to the body of Christ. I really want to encourage any leader in a Christian organization or church to read this book, and consider how both men and women can flourish with their God-given gifts.'

Henriette Engberg Vinkel, KFS Pioneer, Denmark, and psychotherapist in training, Croatia

'The Church is greatly impoverished when women are not identified, equipped and released to use their gifts. All too often, cultural blind spots in the Church have prevented this from happening. I'm thankful that the She Needs blog series has spotlighted these problems and is encouraging the church leaders to be proactive in encouraging women in their church.'

Brian Whittaker, Pastor, Swindon Evangelical Church

Nay Dawson lives in Southampton with the wonderful Jon and two beautiful girls. She is the founder of Passion for Evangelism – a network of creative, public, female evangelists. Nay is a trustee for the Cowrie Scholarship Foundation, raising money for disadvantaged Black British students.

SHE NEEDS

Women flourishing in the Church

Nay Dawson

INTER-VARSITY PRESS
SPCK Group, Studio 101, The Record Hall, 16–16A Baldwin's Gardens, London
EC1N 7RJ, England
Email: ivp@ivpbooks.com
Website: www.ivpbooks.com

First published 2024

British Library Cataloguing-in-Publication Data
A catalogue record for this book is available from the British Library.

ISBN: 978–1–78974–452–1
eBook ISBN: 978–1–78974–453–8

Set in Minion Pro 10.25/13.75pt
Typeset by Fakenham Prepress Solutions, Fakenham, Norfolk NR21 8NL
Printed and bound in Great Britain by Clays Ltd, Elcograf S.p.A.

Produced on paper from sustainable forests

*Inter-Varsity Press publishes Christian books that are true to the Bible and that
communicate the gospel, develop discipleship and strengthen the Church for its
mission in the world.*

*IVP originated within the Inter-Varsity Fellowship, now the Universities and Colleges
Christian Fellowship, a student movement connecting Christian Unions in universities
and colleges throughout Great Britain, and a member movement of the International
Fellowship of Evangelical Students. Website: www.uccf.org.uk. That historic association
is maintained, and all senior IVP staff and committee members subscribe to the UCCF
Basis of Faith.*

To my dear Jon, thank you for walking with me on this painful journey, for holding my head and heart high when all I wanted to do was run away.

With deep gratitude to the brothers who have stood by me from the start: Gareth, David, Dave, Kenny and Malcolm.

To the women of Passion for Evangelism, you bring me such joy and companionship, I would be lost without you.

To my daughters and other young women: I hope this starts a journey of finding your place in the body of Christ.

Contents

Foreword

I'm sad this book had to be written. But I am equally sure that it did.

I guess one risk of a book like this is that some ignore it because they assume it is informed by a particular theological position along the complementarian—egalitarian spectrum. But it actually does not argue one way or the other. It has simply gathered the experiences of the many who responded to Nay Dawson's blogposts and questions. From what I can tell, her correspondents hold a range of different views. But what they share is a sense of pain and confusion derived from their lives in churches over many years. I remember a friend saying a few years ago, ironically enough, that she was surprised to find she was honoured and valued in a complementarian church, far more than she had ever been in her previous egalitarian church. But unfortunately, that does not appear to be common, as we read here.

Other reasons to dismiss the book might also spring quickly to mind. After all, it is a book that exposes painful confusion and pastoral failure and I, for one, found it hard to read at times. It forced me to reflect on my own mistakes and presumptions, on those I had hurt by what I did or didn't do. For too long, our blind spots have perpetuated an unhealthy status quo. But nobody enjoys having their blind spots exposed. So I fear we will make excuses. Perhaps some will blame those raising awkward but legitimate questions, as if they were the problem. We might think that they're too pushy; they have caved in to worldly ambitions or secular agendas; they're not humble or teachable; they're undermining the ministry or even the gospel.

That would be incredibly sad. If only we just stopped to listen carefully to what people are actually saying. Isn't that simply pastoral best practice? Surely, if someone discovers that they have (unwittingly?) contributed to a fellow believer's confusion or hurt, the natural response is to discover how and why. And then to do something about it.

But because so many women have resonated with what Nay has blogged and discussed in recent months, it is obvious that this confusion and hurt is neither isolated nor rare. Many more have shared their experiences with her than could be included in this book, but those who are included are representative. We can't claim to be unaware of how a significant proportion of those in our churches actually feel. Yet many of the things that our sisters have had to endure simply wouldn't be acceptable in any other subsection of Christ's body. As Nay rightly reminds us, we could never imagine Christ himself treating women in this way.

As a result, many women, not to mention the men who love and care for them, will owe Nay a great debt for this brief but important contribution to church life. I certainly hope and pray that it will transform every reader's church or para-church organisation into a more Christlike body that values and creatively nurtures our sisters. Surely, that is not a question of being complementarian or egalitarian. It is a matter of Christian love and service.

Mark Meynell
Director, Europe & Caribbean, Langham Preaching, Langham Partnership

Acknowledgements

Thank you to Kristi and Sarah for always being there to read first drafts and encourage me to be bold and courageous in going ahead to publication!

Thank you to my editor, Tom Creedy, for believing in me enough to commission this book and for your support through my insecurities as I saw it through to completion.

Thank you to Mark Meynell, for your encouragement to keep writing.

Thank you to the women of Passion for Evangelism, for giving me hope and perseverance in the midst of hardship.

Introduction

It all began in Rome. I'd been away for work with a new group of people; the team was global and diverse and made up mostly of women. We talked a lot that week about being women in the Church and in the charities we worked for. What struck me most was that I felt different. They seemed convinced of who they were and felt valued; they knew what God had called them to do and were doing it. They weren't constrained and they didn't compartmentalise who they were in the workplace and who they were in church life. They seemed sure that they had a role to play in the Church and they were doing it. I, however, was in a very different place.

I hadn't always been in that place, but for various reasons I now was. I was unsure how to thrive and flourish both in church and in my workplace, and my confidence and opportunities to serve had hit rock bottom. I left the week full of hope as my eyes had been opened to a whole new world. I arrived at the airport early and decided to browse for articles to read online. The week had made me think a lot and I wanted to read more. In my search, I stumbled across a book called *The Confidence Code*.[1] I was captivated and read the entire book on the way home. I didn't even notice the flight or the train journey; I read and read as quickly as I could. I was amazed that I had found a book that understood me. I found people who felt like me. Finally, after years, I felt as if I had come home.

And so started my journey. A journey of processing and understanding myself and my place in God's mission. The book itself is a great read, it focuses on the art and science of self-assurance in women. The authors combine statistical and anecdotal

---

1 Claire Shipman and Katty Kay, *The Confidence Code: The science and art of self-assurance: What women should know* (New York: Harper Collins, 2014).

evidence and look at factors that have an impact on confidence in women. But why did it take this book to start this journey? Why did it take so many years? If I'm honest I'd listened to influential teachers in churches rather than reading the Bible itself. Only months before, I'd had a conversation with a friend.

He said to me, 'Nay, you're a late bloomer, aren't you?'

I replied, 'What do you mean?'

He continued, 'You've only recently (in your thirties) started giving evangelistic talks.'

I explained. 'When I was 14, inspired by a camp I'd been on, I returned home and set up a Christian Union (CU) at my secondary school. I did this all on my own because I couldn't find another Christian in the school. The CU ran well through the rest of my time and many pupils came along. One year, I asked permission at Easter to run assemblies for my year group. I persuaded friends who didn't go to church to help me out. We did a drama that communicated the cross of Jesus Christ and then I gave a short talk. I explained the drama and invited others to find out more.' I continued to my friend, 'I lost confidence in my early twenties. You've not seen the Nay that I was as a teenager and, yes, it has taken me a while to get that back.'

'Oh,' he said, and the conversation stopped.

I felt very alone.

Finding and reading *The Confidence Code* changed me. I realised that the problem of confidence was not just my issue. It wasn't just I who was a late bloomer, there were others too. The authors interviewed top women from across the world, including heads of state, basketball players, professors and the rest. Each one of them acknowledged that they struggled with confidence. One of those interviewed was Christine Lagarde – a French politician, lawyer and President of the European Central Bank. I was struck that she currently serves as an unofficial counsellor to female leaders around the world. If top female leaders need someone like Christine

Lagarde to counsel them, then surely someone like me needs that too.

I realised in Rome that I had been blind to the potential of women in leadership. I'd begun to think that women didn't really matter in God's mission. *The Confidence Code* showed me that my loss of confidence and my late blooming weren't a showstopper of a problem. And so began a research project that lasted more than five years. I wanted to find out if there were others like me. Others in the Church who lack confidence, others who wonder if they're good enough. I wanted to find out if there were women who struggle to find opportunities to use their gifts. Or women who have hidden talents that they'd love to use but have no role models to learn from. And I wanted to look again at what the Bible says about women and in particular their role in the mission of God.

I've read, written and at each stage interacted with others on social media. I've listened, heard stories and then rewritten in response. In this book, I want to set about exposing what it feels like for many women in the Church. I want to ask questions about where our practice and our theology are misaligned. And I want to get women and their leaders discussing how to bring change. It's important for me that this book is about men and women working alongside one another, hearing one another, and then together discovering a way forward.

One key part to my story is the reading that I've done in community. I lead a network of female evangelists called Passion for Evangelism. Each term, alongside our Greenhouse Mentoring scheme, we read and discuss a book together. Over the three years since we started, we've read a variety of books. We've looked at topical issues addressed by women, books on the role of women in God's mission and evangelistic books by women; I've included the list at the back of this book. It's these books and conversations that have formed my thinking more than anything else. As I've read and discussed with women across the world, I have felt less alone.

As I've read and discussed with others, I've come to pay close attention to Jesus' attitude to women. A recurring theme through many of these books is that Jesus talks a lot about women, that Jesus spends time with women and that Jesus has a crucial and indispensable role for them in his mission. In the first century, many Jewish women were sidelined and marginalised but Jesus valued them: 'Women and slaves were dispossessed but in Greco-Roman culture they could hold meaningful leadership positions in the church.'[2] At times when I've despaired of how women are treated in the Church, I have found solace again and again in the pages and stories of Scripture. I have learnt so much about Jesus through these books. Here are just a few highlights from the Bible that stand out to me...

- Jesus encouraged women to learn (Luke 10:39).
- Jesus gave women a voice (Matthew 28:5–7).
- Jesus appeared first to women (Luke 1).
- Jesus discussed theology with women (John 4).
- Jesus wasn't afraid to spend time with women (Luke 8:1–3).
- Women were key eyewitnesses to the resurrection (Luke 24:1–12).

I'd read many of these verses before, but over the last few years, the scales have dropped from my eyes. I realised that, as a woman, my contribution to the world mattered, my gifts mattered, I realised afresh that I mattered. Karen Soole, in her excellent book, says this about Jesus' encounter with the Samaritan woman: 'This woman mattered; she mattered a lot. Jesus showed time again that women were important to him.'[3]

---

2 Rebecca McLaughlin, *Jesus through the Eyes of Women: How the first female disciples help us know and love the Lord* (Austin, TX: The Gospel Coalition, 2022), p. 11.

3 Karen Soole, *Liberated: How the Bible exalts and dignifies women* (Fearn, Ross-shire: Christian Focus Publications, 2021), Kindle edn, ch. 1.

Working in a para-church organisation and working alongside a variety of church denominations, I had often felt restrained by what women should and shouldn't do both in church and in a para-church setting. Which roles women should and shouldn't take. This confusion led me to question the role of women in God's mission: it's either crucial and indispensable or it isn't. Reading and discussing with other women and the authors of these books helped me greatly. I saw afresh through the encounters found in the New Testament that Jesus values, dignifies and has a role for women.

I mattered to Jesus, but did I matter to his bride?

Even after reading and discussing with others, I still had a big question. I mattered to Jesus, but did I matter to my pastors, my colleagues, the Church, Jesus' bride? One stand-out book that helped me on this was *Worthy: Celebrating the value of women* by Elyse Fitzpatrick and Eric Schumacher.[4] We read it as a group of women and had the opportunity to meet the authors and ask questions. On that night, a friend asked this question: 'I struggle with my role in church, what should I do?' Eric replied, 'Look, pastors are busy people. They have many others to care for and lots of projects to think about. Don't go in demanding their time and loading more on to their plate. Instead, ask them to talk and then explain how this makes you feel.' I'm grateful to Eric for his advice as it set me on a different path. I went and did exactly what he said. I am so grateful to my pastors, their listening ears and their heart to support me.

This book is part of my attempt to apply what Eric suggested but for a wider audience; I want to help others to see how some women

---

4 Elyse Fitzpatrick and Eric Schumacher, *Worthy: Celebrating the value of women* (Bloomington, MN: Bethany House Publishers, 2020).

feel. But not just that. I hope this book can be an aid to conversation between women and their leaders. So, rather than leaders feeling that women are demanding their time and loading more on to their plates, I hope that, if women and their leaders listen to one another and work together, the Church can more truly reflect what it means to be the body of Christ. I'm convinced that women are crucial and indispensable to redemptive history. Yet many women don't know this or experience this in their church. I want to help women and pastors see that women matter in God's mission.

Turn back to the first couple of pages of this book and reread the comments by Jonathan Thomas and Brian Whittaker. These are two friends of mine, male pastors, who share their feelings about approaching the themes in this book. Through this book, I want us to dive into the Bible together and see again some vital aspects of God's vision for the Church and I want us to look at the role women have played and can play in the building up of the Church.

So, let's start with Romans 12:1–8 and the metaphor of the Church as a body.

Therefore, I urge you, brothers and sisters, in view of God's mercy, to offer your bodies as a living sacrifice, holy and pleasing to God – this is your true and proper worship. Do not conform to the pattern of this world but be transformed by the renewing of your mind. Then you will be able to test and approve what God's will is – his good, pleasing and perfect will. For by the grace given me I say to every one of you: Do not think of yourself more highly than you ought, but rather think of yourself with sober judgment, in accordance with the faith God has distributed to each of you. For just as each of us has one body with many members, and these members do not all have the same function, so in Christ we, though many, form one body, and each member belongs to all the others. We have different gifts, according to the grace given to each of us. If your gift is prophesying, then prophesy in accordance with your faith; if it is serving, then serve; if it is teaching, then teach; if it is to encourage, then give encouragement; if it is giving, then give generously; if it is to lead, do it diligently; if it is to show mercy, do it cheerfully.

I used to act as an usher in our local theatre and ended up watching a live showing of The Guilty Feminist podcast. There were six hundred women in the audience and one man; he'd bought the ticket by accident, and he certainly paid for it. I was struck that night, that the general feeling was that the world would be a better place without men. I want to be very clear; this is not what I'm saying. Have a look again at the passage and notice who the passage is addressing and what Paul commends to all of us. Paul opens the section with the phrase 'brothers and sisters'. He talks about how he wants them to work and serve together as members of one body, each of them belonging to one another. This passage, alongside 1 Corinthians 12 and Ephesians 4, is crucial. The only way forward to help women flourish in the Church is for this topic of gifting, service and distribution to be worked out together, as one body, made up of many different parts, but for the building up of the Church.

A question for discussion

Is there space in our churches for women to grow, use and flourish in these gifts or are we stifling women and causing confusion?

This is an important question to find answers to. Are we as broad as the gifting seen in the church in Rome or are we restrictive, over-complicating and causing confusion about what the Bible says? Cynthia Westfall, Assistant Professor of New Testament at McMaster Divinity College in Hamilton, Ontario, says,

The broad spectrum of opinion concerning what exactly is prohibited in what context contributes to the confusion, both for women who are trying to navigate their call and for the churches, and organisations, and individuals who are trying to apply the prohibition.[5]

Clarity is essential and, ultimately, it's kind.

Reading *The Confidence Code* showed me a world of women who, although highly talented and competent, were still insecure and under-confident in their abilities. This somehow made them more imitable, more like role models than I'd ever seen before. In the New Testament, you see women as co-workers, disciples and sisters. So why did it take *The Confidence Code* to highlight to me what has always been in Scripture?

I wonder if, first of all, it's common grace. Charles Hodge, nineteenth-century Reformed theologian, described it like this:

The Holy Spirit as the Spirit of truth, of holiness, and of life in all its forms, is present with every human mind, enforcing truth, restraining from evil, exciting to good, and imparting wisdom or strength, when, where, and in what measure seemeth to Him good.[6]

I also wonder if the hopes and dreams about how women can serve the Church really aren't talked about very much.

I was once told, 'Nay, you should stop talking about women using their gifts in the Church; they, like everyone else, just need to get on and serve where there is a need.' That certainly stopped me in my tracks. Was I wrong to encourage women in an area of

---

5 Cynthia L. Westfall, *Paul and Gender: Reclaiming the apostle's vision for men and women in Christ* (Grand Rapids, MI: Baker Academic, 2016), Kindle edn, ch. 7.

6 Charles Hodge, *Systematic Theology*, vol. 2 (Grand Rapids, MI: Eerdmans, 1940), p. 486.

unused, unspotted gifting? Was I wrong to see untapped potential in female friends? I saw something in *The Confidence Code* of the Proverbs 31 woman. I saw a woman engaged in business, society and culture and it reminded me of this remarkable biblical figure. A woman for whom it was said, 'Many women do noble things, but you surpass them all' (Proverbs 31:29). Yet, sadly, unlike my colleagues in Rome, I had compartmentalised who I was in my church life, my home life and my work life. I'm grateful that the Spirit awakened me through reading this book and led me back with a heart ready to hear.

Why there is more to this than this book

I set up Passion for Evangelism (PfE) because I want to see women alongside men recognise and use the evangelistic gifts they have to build up the Church. For me, how women and men work together is an important message to the watching world and says something about what we believe about God. As women and men proclaim the gospel together, we have an opportunity to show the world what restored, sibling relationships look like. Men and women working together in evangelism adorns the gospel and points to a better story!

I find that there is nothing more exciting than seeing a need, seeing someone who can help and encouraging them to get involved. Over the years, I've seen so many women get involved with PfE. They arrive under-confident, often rusty and unsure about their gifts; many of them struggle to find their place in the Church. I am so happy when they write to me a year or two later. The message usually goes like this: 'Nay, my time serving in PfE is up. I've got so busy serving in the local church that something needs to give. Would you mind if I give up being on the PfE team?' My response each time is: 'I'm delighted, go guilt free and serve.' And then I thank God that we've played our small part in the rebooting of women, giving them hope, mentoring and opportunities. It's wonderful to see women rediscovering their gifts and using them to build up their church.

As you read this book, it will open some raw conversations. Please don't shy away from these or leave the discussion too soon. My hope and prayer is that, in time, these conversations will lead women and men to work together as one body. We need to learn to listen to one another, understand one another and work together. This book is intended to be read together, so why not start as you mean to go on and buy a second copy for someone else in your church. 'Would you join me?'

She doesn't feel good enough to serve in your church

> 'Men apply for a job when they meet just 60% of the qualifications, but women apply only if they meet 100% of them.'
> (Hewlett Packard internal report[1])

> ...those parts of the body that seem to be weaker are indispensable.
> (1 Corinthians 12:22)

Have you ever worked down a list of personal attributes required in a job advert, treating it like a checklist?

Yes, yes, yes, no, no, MOVE ON.

Yes, yes, yes, no, no, APPLY.

This is the average experience of women and men applying for jobs. Research shows that men apply for a job when they meet just 60% of the qualifications. Women, on the other hand, tend to apply only if they meet 100% of them. As you read these statistics, I wonder if they ring true for your experience? Maybe not for you, but it's worth asking a few of your friends and seeing what they think. When applying for a job or a voluntary role, what percentage of the qualifications did you feel you needed before you applied? Why is this and why is there such a difference between men and women?

The statistic above from Hewlett Packard has been discussed, debated and challenged. Is this about confidence, a mistaken

---

1   Claire Shipman and Katty Kay, *The Confidence Code: The science and art of self-assurance: What women should know* (New York: Harper Collins, 2014), p. 21.

perception of the hiring process, or is it about women not wanting to waste anyone's time? What doesn't seem to be questioned, though, is whether the statistics are true and, if so, what impact this has on women.

It seems that women have issues in putting themselves forward, but not just for jobs. Research shows that the same is true for requesting a pay rise, speaking up in public settings and bouncing back from failure. On top of this, many worry that they are not sufficiently qualified for the job in hand and so simply don't apply. A McKinsey report says, 'On average women view 25% more jobs before making an application than a man.'[2] Ironically, in this same research, they discovered that women did 35% better than men at interviews.

The implications of the research from Hewlett Packard are widespread. But, for me, I want to apply it to the flourishing of men and women in everyday church life. These statistics aren't just job-related. The same can be applied to projects at work, church, a volunteer role, or a great idea that you'd love to see happen. How many times have you written off an opportunity, not applied for something or not volunteered yourself? And why is this?

Many people feel that they need to be 100% perfect or competent before they offer themselves. This could be to lead a Bible study in a homegroup, speak at an evangelistic course, share a testimony at the front of church or any other type of service. I asked friends to give some examples of what this 100% perfection looks like for them. Here are three different responses:

Laura
I think that often, as women, we compare ourselves to standards and expectations that are created by men or expected of men,

---

2   Alexis Krivkovich et al. 'Women in the Workplace', McKinsey and Company, 18 October 2022: https://www.mckinsey.com/featured-insights/diversity-and-inclusion/women-in-the-workplace (accessed 12 September 2023).

rather than ones that allow for our giftings and different approaches to tasks.

Matt

This is a big issue and one I care passionately about. Although I am a researcher in all things men and church, I'm also a dad of a second-year undergraduate at a top university. Despite her being academically very bright, she still, in her own words, lacks confidence. She will often talk of a culture of patriarchy, despite her course being 80% women – as is often the case in humanities, medicine and increasingly the law. I'm sure many men may just naturally feel an impulse to jump in with a first question – I'm guilty – because many of us think aloud and it's our way of processing what we've heard.

Sarah

There's also a sense in which you 'can't be what you can't see' – it's self-fulfilling. If there's rarely a woman at the front of church, you'll subconsciously believe that women are no good at doing those things, and that makes you less likely to do it yourself.

In my discussions of this over the years with women, three phrases keep emerging. I'm going to call them the three myths. It seems as if there is one problem undergirded by three myths. The problem is that women are less likely to put themselves forward than men. The three myths are:

- the myth of perfectionism – God can only use perfection;
- the myth of being second-best – someone else can do it better;
- the myth of headhunting – gifted people are headhunted.

Here are three friends. You'll see that the three myths appear in their stories:

Andrea loves to write. She read the original blog series out of which this book was born and wrote a thoughtful and articulate response. Despite the fact that it was well written and a useful addition to the series, she never sent it. She says, 'My thoughts never felt well articulated or fully formed so I never got around to sending them.'

Rachel is a gifted woman. Whenever she prays in church, she points to Christ in a way that teaches me afresh. I talked with her and asked her if she would consider giving a short testimony at church, but she said she could never do this. I asked why not. She replied, 'Because it takes me so long to prepare.' She asked, 'Surely someone who is really gifted wouldn't take that long or be that nervous before delivering a testimony?'

Emma loves communicating the gospel in public. She felt free to do it as a teenager, but the church she attended as an adult didn't have any women who offered teaching. Groups of men were encouraged and trained to speak; she wasn't. She longed to be invited to speak at the Christmas evangelistic event, but she just didn't have the courage to ask. She was worried that if they said no she'd have to live with the embarrassment of overreaching herself.

Are you like Andrea, Rachel or Emma? Do you have women like this in your church? How could you encourage them and help them to grow and build up the church?

Imagine this scenario: a new team is formed for running and planning an evangelistic course. Those attending church are invited to join as cooks, welcomers and table leaders but the speakers have already been chosen. Andrea has written some excellent discussion questions to be used but wonders if they're good enough to show the church leader. The pastor asks Rachel to give her testimony and she says no. Emma loves communicating the gospel and would love to be asked. How could you find out what these women genuinely feel and encourage them and help them to grow and get involved in this outreach?

Many churches and organisations can have cultures of favouritism and elitism. New teams are formed with no thought of someone like Andrea, Rachel or Emma. The cycle is perpetuated, and the inner voice of courage squashed and replaced with, 'See, this really isn't something I could do.' At this point, you might think I'm exaggerating. I can honestly say I've felt all these things.

If women are less likely to offer themselves, then we need to be more proactive in inviting women to get involved. But it's more complex than that. Good friends of mine who lead churches and conferences have spoken with me, frustrated that they've tried to get women involved and been met, each time, with a firm 'No'. Sadly, it's just not as simple as inviting women to get involved. We need to offer mentoring, training and feedback along the way.

But why bother with this? Why focus on this subject? Like me, you may have encountered plenty of discouragement. Friends have said to me, 'It's not about confidence; women are just being disobedient to their calling.' Others have said, 'Women, like men, should serve where there are needs, not obsess about using certain gifts.' Why bother with getting half of the image of God involved in sharing about him? Let's have a look together at 1 Corinthians 12:1–26.

One of the key metaphors for the Church is that of a body. A body made up of many parts, yet each is different. Each part is given gifts by the Spirit to build up the Church. Each part is not just welcomed, but essential. Each part is sure of their purpose and convinced of their value.

> Now about the gifts of the Spirit, brothers and sisters, I do not want you to be uninformed. You know that when you were

pagans, somehow or other you were influenced and led astray to dumb idols. Therefore I want you to know that no one who is speaking by the Spirit of God says, 'Jesus be cursed,' and no one can say, 'Jesus is Lord,' except by the Holy Spirit.

There are different kinds of gifts, but the same Spirit distributes them. There are different kinds of service, but the same Lord. There are different kinds of working, but in all of them and in everyone it is the same God at work.

Now to each one the manifestation of the Spirit is given for the common good. To one there is given through the Spirit a message of wisdom, to another a message of knowledge by means of the same Spirit, to another faith by the same Spirit, to another gifts of healing by that one Spirit, to another miraculous powers, to another prophecy, to another distinguishing between spirits, to another speaking in different kinds of tongues, and to still another the interpretation of tongues. All these are the work of one and the same Spirit, and he distributes them to each one, just as he determines.

Just as a body, though one, has many parts, but all its many parts form one body, so it is with Christ. For we were all baptized by one Spirit so as to form one body – whether Jews or Gentiles, slave or free – and we were all given the one Spirit to drink. Even so the body is not made up of one part but of many.

Now if the foot should say, 'Because I am not a hand, I do not belong to the body,' it would not for that reason stop being part of the body. And if the ear should say, 'Because I am not an eye, I do not belong to the body,' it would not for that reason stop being part of the body. If the whole body were an eye, where would the sense of hearing be? If the whole body were an ear, where would the sense of smell be? But in fact God has placed the parts in the body, every one of them, just as he wanted them to be. If they were all one part, where would the body be? As it is, there are many parts, but one body.

The eye cannot say to the hand, 'I don't need you!' And the head cannot say to the feet, 'I don't need you!' On the contrary, those parts of the body that seem to be weaker are indispensable, and the parts that we think are less honourable we treat with special honour. And the parts that are unpresentable are treated with special modesty, while our presentable parts need no special treatment. But God has put the body together, giving greater honour to the parts that lacked it, so that there should be no division in the body, but that its parts should have equal concern for each other. If one part suffers, every part suffers with it; if one part is honoured, every part rejoices with it.

What a vision for the Church. A fully functioning healthy body, working together for the good of the body (v. 13), brought together through the Spirit of Christ. Yet, for many, this vision is so far from their reality. So many women wonder how to use the gifts God has given them to serve in the local church and many others turn to para-church ministries. Let's stop for a moment and imagine a local church, full of people with diverse gifts, celebrating and encouraging each other and working alongside each other as brothers and sisters in Christ.

It's so easy to fall into the trap of thinking of 'giftedness' as our own human ability to do things well. Instead, we need to get into the habit of seeing gifts as given by the Spirit, arranged by Christ, received in Christ and used for the Lord Jesus.

There are women in our churches gifted by the Spirit. Can we really say to one another, 'I don't need you!'? The church body is given different gifts but by the same Spirit. There are different acts of service but done for the same Lord Jesus.

Over the past twenty years, I have seen many women, trained and gifted, who are not using certain gifts to build up the local church. Take, for example, Anna. She loves reading theology, understanding big concepts and explaining them clearly. What is her future in her church? Well, it would be OK if she wanted to lead kids' work, or sing in the band or be on the prayer team. But what about her passion and giftings? I want to be clear here: the examples I give are women who are rooted in and committed to their church; all of them are serving where there is need and opportunity. However, almost all would say that they are not using some of their *unique* gifts to build up the Church.

What does this passage say about the three myths and the problem of not offering yourself?

Could it be as simple as women learning to offer themselves or volunteer for something they'd really like to do? For some, maybe. Becca got in touch to say:

> I read your blog post and identified a lot with it. I had a friend who didn't feel good enough to apply for a job. So, I sent it to her to read, along with a few messages of support. Thanks to your article and a nudge from God for me to encourage her, she went for a job she wouldn't have gone for and got it!!

Maybe that story is all you need. Why not give it a go, put your idea forward, offer yourself to your pastor and your local community and see what happens? Action can lead to confidence and the more we try the more we'll have opportunities. But to help you along the way, be sure to invite others to walk alongside you in this journey.

But for others, perhaps most of us, the words in 1 Corinthians will feel really apt. Here you see the inner monologue of the body parts comparing themselves with each other: "'Because I am not a hand, I do not belong to the body"...And if the ear should say, "Because I am not an eye, I do not belong to the body.'"

I can just imagine the body parts saying, 'I'm not good enough, I'm not as talented, I don't have their gifts, I'm not needed.' Yet the beauty of the metaphor is one of diversity and inclusion. Diversity of the body parts and inclusion of all the parts. The metaphor of the body is not just a nice ideal, it's essential to the communication of the gospel. Gordon Fee says of this passage, 'All members are necessary if there is to be a body and not a monstrosity.'[3] It's in that diversity and welcome, in the cross-cultural, unnatural friendships, that something of Christ's body is seen. Does your church body reflect a fully functioning body? Does your church body image Christ's body? Or is it a monstrosity?

The myth of perfectionism – God can only use perfection

Maybe one of the reasons why women feel this is because they don't feel good enough or skilled enough for God to use them. Not only do they lack confidence, but they also have no experience in the process of preparing. There are so many things that hold women back from serving God. For many, they feel as if they need to be 100% perfect at everything they do to serve God, rather than trusting that God delights to work with flawed and broken people.

Peter rebuked Jesus, fell asleep on him and denied him, yet this same Peter was reinstated as his friend and was used mightily by God. In Matthew 16:18, Jesus makes clear the central role Simon Peter will play in establishing his Church, emphasising again the name Peter, 'Rock', that Jesus chose to give him. The cross and resurrection show us forgiveness and restoration both for us and in our service of our local church. The early Church was built upon a

---

3   Gordon Fee, *The First Epistle to the Corinthians*, The New International Commentary on the New Testament (Grand Rapids, MI: Eerdmans, 2014), p. 609.

person who was not perfect, so we too do not need to be perfect as we offer ourselves to build up the local church.

The myth of being second-best – someone else can do it better

This chapter allows us to imagine the body parts wishing they were another part of the body or believing that they aren't any good. There will always be someone better than you, but there is only you placed in your church, your family, your workplace. Verse 18 says, 'But in fact God has placed the parts in the body, every one of them, just as he wanted them to be.'

The myth of headhunting – gifted people are headhunted

I have spent so much time thinking that if I'm good enough at what I do, someone will notice and ask me to get involved; they will send me an invite for a job or ask me to speak at a conference. In cultures where favourites get chosen and appointed, it is easy to believe that headhunting is the only way in which God can work. In reading this passage again in the light of this discussion, we see that it is the Spirit who is the headhunter, not the pastor, manager or director. It seems we have forgotten that gifts are given by the Spirit (v. 1) and those gifts are given to build up the Church. If you're unsure what your gifts and talents are, then ask those around you or take some time to do a Strengths Finder Test. James Lawrence says simply:

> The good news is that nearly everyone develops talents as they grow up, although sometimes they are a little harder to identify due to certain life experiences. Another way of thinking of these talents is that they aren't what you can do, but what you can't help yourself doing.[4]

---

4 James Lawrence, *Growing Leaders: Reflections on leadership, life and Jesus* (Abingdon: Bible Reading Fellowship, 2020), p. 526.

Maybe some have the privilege in life to be sought after, schmoozed and chased until they sign on the dotted line. But that only takes away from the truth that it's the Spirit who gives and distributes the gifts.

It is the Spirit who gives gifts, gifts that are tools not jewels, gifts that build up the Church of God. This week, have a go at offering yourself for a project, serve in a new capacity or share the good news of Jesus with a friend, even if you only feel 60% good enough or 60% ready.

These chapters are written to start a conversation. My hope is that, together, women and their leaders will read, listen and discuss a way forward. Here are some questions to start with.

Questions for discussion

- Which of these real-life stories rings true for you?
- Which of the myths do you identify with the most and why:
  - the myth of perfectionism – God can only use perfection;
  - the myth of being second-best – someone else can do it better;
  - the myth of headhunting – gifted people are headhunted?
- As brothers and sisters, how can we work together to mentor women, come alongside them and find opportunities for them to flourish?

She needs help failing

The propensity to dwell on failure and mistakes, and an inability to shut out the outside world are the biggest psychological impediments for female players.
(Mike Thibault, Mystics basketball coach[1])

'And I tell you that you are Peter, and on this rock I will build my church, and the gates of Hades will not overcome it.'
(Matthew 16:18)

Mike Thibault was a legendary basketball coach. Over the years, he coached men and women to National Basketball Association (NBA) level, the highest level of greatness in basketball. Katty Kay and Claire Shipman conducted an interview with him for their book *The Confidence Code*. Mike observed the differences between the male and female players, and the results were surprising. He says:

Even in one of the most aggressive and challenging professional sports that women can play there was still a clear difference. If the female players had a bad game, they would say something like… 'oh my gosh, we lost, and I really wanted to help the team win, and win for the fans'. With guys, if they had a bad game, they're thinking 'I have had a bad game' and they shrug off the loss more quickly.

---

1   Claire Shipman and Katty Kay, *The Confidence Code: The science and art of self-assurance: What women should know* (New York: Harper Collins, 2014), p. 5.

It's been said that, after making a mistake on court, it takes men a couple of hours to bounce back, whereas for women it's more like two weeks.[2]

Failure and rejection are part of life, and yet our inability to handle them is a massive drawback. When something goes wrong, women can feel that they have failed in some way. This could be over-thinking, internalising setbacks or replaying mistakes. According to this anecdotal research, women can be more influenced by negative feedback and struggle to bounce back from failure. Here is another example of how women find failure harder to deal with than men.

Harvard economics professor Claudia Goldin found out that male economics majors outnumber women by almost 3:1.[3] She discovered that women who earn below an A in introductory economics classes are far more likely than their male peers to switch courses to a different major. According to her analysis, women who earned Bs were half as likely as those who earned As to stick with the major. But their male classmates weren't nearly so dissuaded: a man who earned a B was just as likely to major in economics as a man who earned an A. The summary is that women are less likely to major in the field if, in their first course, they don't do well.

These, like all the other statistics, are generalisations, and maybe for you this isn't about a clear gender split; however, there are many for whom it will make sense to see it in this way. For women, they will have already found it harder to offer themselves just to get in the game. But once they're in, once they've mustered up the courage to put themselves forward, they're still going to need help. And when failure comes, it is going to take women

2 Shipman and Kay, *The Confidence Code*, p. 4.

3 Claudia Goldin, 'Gender and the Undergraduate Economics Major', Department of Economics, Harvard University, 12 April 2015: https://scholar.harvard.edu/files/goldin/files/claudia_gender_paper.pdf?m=1429198526 (accessed 13 September 2023).

longer to recover than one may think. Some never recover and may just simply walk away. I resonate strongly with Mike Thibault's comments.

I regularly do talks at Christian Unions and, after delivering them, it can take me a long time to recover. I sometimes have a deep sense of failure and shame, and I question myself and my ability. It's easy to wonder if someone else could do a better job than I can, and I will regularly tell myself to say no next time. When my husband suggests I ask for feedback about a talk, I often avoid it in case it's too crushing.

I wanted to find out if I was the only one who felt like this, so I asked friends for some examples of failure. Here is what they had to say.

Hannah shared about her experience of failure at work: 'When I first started at my current job, if we missed out on a grant that I thought we should have got, I would often go to bed for a week. The inability to deal with failure was overwhelming.'

Alice shared how the potential to fail holds her back: 'I think we feel as if we need to be 100% perfect at everything we do in order to serve God, rather than trusting that God delights to work with flawed and broken people such as you and me.'

For many women, there is the added pressure of being a pioneer and being the first woman to do the task. Anna talks about the failure she feels when doing something for the first time:

Women are rarely seen teaching or leading a service, or in preaching roles in churches. So, when a woman stands up, she is very noticeable as a woman in that role; she's not just another guy at the front like every other Sunday. So, that one sermon or talk can really colour people's opinions and expectations of all women in that same role. You become the representative of all the women in the Church, whether you like it or not.

These are real problems for many women. Friends have commented on how they are learning to live with a less-than-perfect expectation of themselves. For one friend, this meant submitting essays for her course without spending excessive amounts of time editing repeatedly. For another friend, it meant asking for feedback from others and being brave enough to read it.

So how can we help women to flourish? My friend Dave says this:

Failure is unavoidable and baked into Christianity. How we help one another come back from it is massive. Failure often eats me up, so I take seriously these insights that women generally find failure harder than men. How will we help one another?

What do Hannah, Alice and Anna need?

Months on, Hannah is still in the same job; she's had fewer days in bed and seems generally happier. I asked what had made the difference. She replied, 'Now I have an amazing manager who constantly tells me how great I am and, funnily enough, these days I cope much better with failure!' Her boss knows that she particularly thrives on encouragement, and it's worked. She's brought in grants, is content and works well in a team.

For many women, a lack of opportunities holds them back from serving with certain gifts. But for Anna, there's a different problem. She has been asked to give an evangelistic talk, but it's the first time a woman has done this in her setting. As she prepares, she feels that she has the double whammy of honouring God and the church in her preparation, but she is also conscious of what others might feel about her. As everyone is so different, it is worth asking what would actually help her in this process. Here are some ideas:

- Offer to pray when she sits down to prepare.
- Give feedback on her script.

- Sit on the front row during the talk.
- Encourage her during the talk by being genuinely attentive.
- Take her out for lunch afterwards for distraction and encouragement.
- Ask her how it feels to be the first woman to give such a talk.

We are to serve wholeheartedly, as if we are serving the Lord, not people. But when you are the first person ever to do something, you'll need a lot more help and support in doing this. I have often been the first, I love having ideas and implementing them, but there are times when I get really scared. Texts from friends, feedback on my script, prayer beforehand, encouraging words afterwards: all these things have helped me.

So how do we create a culture and environment where women can grow in resilience and bounce back from failure?

The New Testament metaphor for the Church as a body is essential here. As we saw in chapter 1, gifts are given to each part to build up the body of the Church. But it's also the Church, the body, that creates the environment and culture for men and women to work as siblings, co-workers and co-heirs together. So that, as Dave says above, we learn to help one another and create a culture where each person flourishes. Studies show that much time and thought has been poured into helping elite athletes to grow in resilience. You might laugh and think, 'I'm so far from being an elite athlete; how can this help?' but stick with me.

The chart opposite is inspired by the Challenge–Support matrix by Fletcher and Sarkar.[4] It shows that the most conducive environment for athletes is a facilitative environment. This is an environment with high support and high challenge. But what about

---

4 Dr Mustafa Sarkar, 'Developing Resilience in Elite Sport: The Role of the Environment', *The Sport and Exercise Scientist*, 11 April 2021: https://www.bases.org.uk/imgs/55_tses_editor_s_choice_spread__p20_21_815.pdf (accessed 13 September 2023).

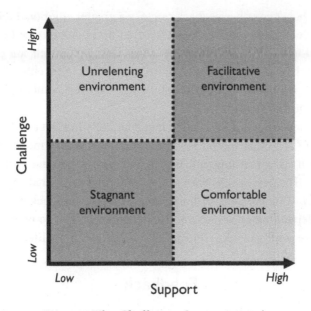

Figure 1 **The Challenge–Support matrix**

the other environments? As you can see there is a mixture of low/ high support and low/high challenge, resulting in environments described as unrelenting, stagnant or comfortable.

The swimming club that my daughters belong to is an environment that provides great support from teammates, other parents and in particular Marie, their coach. But it's not just the support that creates a facilitative environment, it's the fresh challenge. Whether that's the skins race once they turn 11, which operates on a knockout basis whereby they race until one swimmer is left, or whether it's the chance to chase times for the counties, there always seem to be new challenges. Elite athletes learn how not to be afraid of failure. They learn how to get back up.

But back to women in the Church, how do you help women not to be afraid of failure? How do you help women learn how to get back up? Especially because some find positive feedback too hard to stomach, yet negative feedback can take a greater emotional toil. As you reflect upon your life as a Christian and your service in your local church, there will be times when your failure felt too great. Rather than focusing on the failure, let's look at how elite athletes develop resilience and performance through the combination of challenge and support.

Resilience is a hot topic at the moment, but what is it and how do we get it? It is often viewed as a fixed trait, but it's much more helpful to see it as something influenced by a range of environmental factors. The key to resilience is the combination of challenge and support. This happens in four ways, through: feedback, giving it a go, depending on others and challenging yourself to be fearless. Here are some examples of what this looks like in my life.

Feedback

I lead a network of female evangelists. We regularly run a mentoring scheme called The Greenhouse. Over five weeks, women create evangelistic content: a song, a short story for kids, a blog or a video for social media. In small groups, we give peer feedback that seeks to improve how well they identify and invite others and persuade them to find out more about Jesus. Here is what one friend said about The Greenhouse: 'Women play a crucial role in the contemporary Church. That's why they need to be given wings to fly. That's what PfE and the Greenhouse mentoring scheme have given to me.'

Giving it a go

This is often the thing that holds most of my friends back. They've got material (a talk, a blog or a song) but they just don't have opportunities to test and use it, to grow in and serve with some of the gifts they have. The lack of opportunities has a disproportional effect on courage: ironically, it's been found that regular opportunities would grow confidence and courage. I'm regularly reminded that women should 'just get on and serve where there is a need', and I certainly don't disagree with that. As a family, we love our local church and are willing and available to serve where there is need. But, saying all this, many women find that certain gifts they have, usually leadership and teaching gifts, become underused and even treated as suspect within their local church. Friends who have worked for three to five years in a ministry apprentice scheme find at the end that the pathway is clear for men but for women it's a dead end. This begs many questions, such as:

- What were we trained for?
- Why do I have these skills?
- And why does my church not recognise these gifts?

For women with no formal training, some will have an inkling of a gifting, or a desire to serve in a particular way, but when there are few or no role models, it's hard to imagine what could be done or how to do it.

I'm constantly refreshed when I read the Bible and see that women are crucial and indispensable to God's mission. However, for those of us who aren't pioneers, we need to see someone else do it first before we know how to do it or feel that we are allowed to join in. This is where women need you to open the door for them, find them an opportunity, expose them to role models, be an encourager and enable them to give it a go.

Sadly, this isn't the experience of many. Sally found that, despite asking her pastor for opportunities to serve, grow and build up the church with her gifts, it was only through her initiating and setting up a new ministry that she was able to flourish. On one level, this is great, but it does leave her in doubt as to whether the church wants her to be doing this. She asked some searching questions. 'Is this really a church ministry? What level of support, accountability and encouragement can I expect if I've set this up on my own?'

Lisa worked for two years as a ministry apprentice and is now a teacher. She says this:

> For me, it was more about the lack of opportunity and the lack of conversation around the opportunities for women in ministry. I've also since realised that a children's worker isn't the only role I could have been suited to. But in the type of church I was in, it felt like the only option for a woman like me. If one of my church leaders had had a serious discussion with me about my options, I might have realised this at the time!!

Depending on others

The New Testament is brimming with teamwork, encouragement and support of one another. A quick read through Romans 16 shows partnership, friendship and like-mindedness. Paul lists so many people, men and women from all walks of life. It's this level of brotherly and sisterly partnership in the gospel that is essential for women to flourish in the Church. I've got friends with whom I chat regularly; we talk about the highs and lows of being a woman and wanting to serve our church. I've got male friends who get in touch and encourage me. My husband and friends speak truth and encouragement to me when I need it the most. We have to find others with whom we can be honest and on whom we can lean, people who can also lean on us.

Challenging yourself to be fearless

My friend Christine was asked to give a model evangelistic talk at a conference, but she replied, 'I'd rather not do it. I'm feeling a bit rusty at the moment, and there are others who could do this far better than me. I'd much prefer to sit in the audience and listen.' How can we help Christine to exercise her gift? It's got to include helping her to grow in confidence and courage. The planning team went back to her, explaining why she was equipped and suited to do this. They explained that they didn't want her to sit in the audience; they wanted to hear what she had to say.

Women will often refuse an invite and will need more encouragement, validation or persuasion before they can agree to do something. I have had numerous conversations like this:

- N Hi Edith, would you consider leading a mentoring group for The Greenhouse?
- E Thanks, Nay, really honoured that you asked me, but this isn't for me.
- N Why's that?
- E I haven't got time...
- N Any other reason?
- E I'm not sure I've got the experience to do it.
- N From what I've seen of you, I think you'll be great, and we'll give you all the support you need.
- E But I've not been trained like the others.

I usually then reply by asking, 'Could we talk?' I want to find out what is holding her back. Is it really a lack of time or is it something else? In the PfE Greenhouse mentoring scheme, we focus on women's character because we recognise that, for women, publicly proclaiming Jesus comes with some nervousness. We think and pray over how understanding the truth of the gospel helps you to take a risk.

We have seen so far that God has given gifts to both men and women to serve the Church. And yet, in many churches, women are struggling to use gifts bestowed by the Spirit. I've given some ideas for how to encourage women in this. But, most importantly, women need to know how to fail well.

Let's look at someone who failed, someone through whom God chose to work to help him build the early Church. Let's look at what the Bible says about failure through the life of Peter. Read these verses and reflect on the words you would use to describe Peter.

'But what about you?' he asked. 'Who do you say I am?'

Peter answered, 'You are the Messiah.'

Jesus warned them not to tell anyone about him.

He then began to teach them that the Son of Man must suffer many things and be rejected by the elders, the chief priests and the teachers of the law, and that he must be killed and after three days rise again. He spoke plainly about this, and Peter took him aside and began to rebuke him.

But when Jesus turned and looked at his disciples, he rebuked Peter. 'Get behind me, Satan!' he said. 'You do not have in mind the concerns of God, but merely human concerns.'

(Mark 8:29–33)

Peter declared, 'Even if all fall away, I will not.'

'Truly I tell you,' Jesus answered, 'today – yes, tonight – before the cock crows twice you yourself will disown me three times.'

But Peter insisted emphatically, 'Even if I have to die with you, I will never disown you.' And all the others said the same.

They went to a place called Gethsemane, and Jesus said to his disciples, 'Sit here while I pray.' He took Peter, James and John along with him, and he began to be deeply distressed and troubled. 'My soul is overwhelmed with sorrow to the point of death,' he said to them. 'Stay here and keep watch.'

Going a little farther, he fell to the ground and prayed that, if possible, the hour might pass from him. '*Abba*, Father,' he said, 'everything is possible for you. Take this cup from me. Yet not what I will, but what you will.'

Then he returned to his disciples and found them sleeping. 'Simon,' he said to Peter, 'are you asleep? Couldn't you keep watch for one hour? Watch and pray so that you will not fall into temptation. The spirit is willing, but the flesh is weak.'

Once more he went away and prayed the same thing. When he came back, he again found them sleeping, because their eyes were heavy. They did not know what to say to him.

Returning the third time, he said to them, 'Are you still sleeping and resting? Enough! The hour has come. Look, the Son of Man is delivered into the hands of sinners. Rise! Let us go! Here comes my betrayer!'
(Mark 14:29–42)

While Peter was below in the courtyard, one of the servant-girls of the high priest came by. When she saw Peter warming himself, she looked closely at him.

'You also were with that Nazarene, Jesus,' she said.

But he denied it. 'I don't know or understand what you're talking about,' he said, and went out into the entrance.

When the servant-girl saw him there, she said again to those standing round them, 'This fellow is one of them.' Again he denied it.

After a little while, those standing near said to Peter, 'Surely you are one of them, for you are a Galilean.'

He began to call down curses, and he swore to them, 'I don't know this man you're talking about.'

> Immediately the cock crowed the second time. Then Peter remembered the word Jesus had spoken to him: 'Before the cock crows twice you will disown me three times.' And he broke down and wept.
> (Mark 14:66–72)

Throughout Mark's Gospel, we see the real Peter. Here are some lowlights from the passages above:

- publicly proclaiming that Jesus is the Messiah (8:29);
- publicly stating that he would never deny Jesus (14:29, 31);
- rebuking Jesus in front of others (8:32);
- being rebuked by Jesus (8:33);
- being called Satan by Jesus (8:33);
- falling asleep on Jesus three times (14:37, 40, 41);
- disowning Jesus three times (14:68, 70, 71–2).

Reading this feels like an exhausting list of failures. If you were leading a project at church, would you choose Peter to be on your team? If you were Peter, would you have offered yourself to be on a team at this point?

But this failure isn't the end of the story. Peter's life is a life of grace and growth. The life of discipleship isn't meant to be stagnant, but one of growth. Later, Peter is described as the rock on which the early Church was built (Matthew 16:18) and history tells us that the early Church grew 40% per decade for nearly three centuries. So, what happened to Peter? How was this passionate, impetuous, fickle person transformed into a rock?

Between chapters 14 and 16 in Mark's Gospel, we see the death and resurrection of Peter's friend, his Messiah. But we also see the words from the angel: go and tell the disciples and Peter. The reinstatement of Peter shows us that God stretches out his hands not only in rescuing Peter but also in using Peter's failure to build his Church.

Peter, the one who denied him, fell asleep on him and even rebuked him was reinstated as his friend. Imagine the sheer relief at the inclusion and singling out of his name. God chooses to use people who are far from perfect, and the inclusion of Peter's name displays the nature of God. His generous grace and kindness in working through people such as you and me. The cross and resurrection show us forgiveness and restoration both for us personally and in our ministry. I wonder if lesson number one for women to learn is that God does not expect perfection from those who follow him. If God can work through someone such as Peter, then surely you and I are not out of the picture either? And when we do fail, we must remember what Jesus said to Peter before his failure: 'But I have prayed for you, Simon, that your faith may not fail. And when you have turned back, strengthen your brothers' (Luke 22:32).

Jon Bloom says this about failure:

Peter was going to sin – miserably. But Jesus had prayed for him. Jesus' prayer was stronger than Peter's sin, and it's stronger than our sin too …

Peter's failure did not define him. And ours will not define us. They are horrible, humbling stumbles along the path of following Jesus, who paid for them all on the cross.

And Jesus specialises in transforming failures into rocks of strength for his church.[5]

Jesus chooses and uses failures such as you and me, but let's do all we can to help women in their failure to flourish in our church.

---

5   Jon Bloom, 'Jesus Chooses and Uses Failures', The Gospel Coalition, 3 February 2012: https://www.desiringgod.org/articles/jesus-chooses-and-uses-failures--2 (accessed 13 September 2023).

Questions for discussion

- Using the principles of support and challenge, how could you encourage a culture of growth?
- Think of a situation where you 'failed'. What did your reaction to this failure look like? How long did it take you to bounce back from it? What hope do you draw from Peter's story?

She needs help speaking

Women, when outnumbered, spoke as much as 75 percent less than men.[1]

'Then go quickly and tell his disciples: "He has risen from the dead and is going ahead of you into Galilee."'
(Matthew 28:7)

One Princeton research team set out to measure how much less women talk. Male and female volunteers were put to work solving a budget challenge. The study found that in some cases women, when in the minority, spoke 75% less than men did.[2] But it's not just speaking. According to this research in *The Economist*:

Men are disproportionately more likely to ask the first question at a seminar. If a man has asked the first question – men are then more than twice as likely to ask a question afterwards. But when a woman asks the first question, men and women both ask around 50% of questions afterwards.[3]

This article highlights the inconsistency inherent in men and women asking questions in seminar groups.

---

1 Joseph G. Hadfield, 'Women Speak Up Less When They're Outnumbered', Y Magazine, 10 August 2023: https://magazine.byu.edu/article/women-speak-up-less-when-theyre-outnumbered/ (accessed 13 September 2023).

2 Christopher F. Karpowitz et al., 'Gender Inequality in Deliberative Participation', American Political Science Review, 9 August 2012: https://doi.org/10.1017/S0003055412000329 (accessed 13 September 2023).

3 'Women Ask Fewer Questions Than Men', The Economist, 7 December 2017: https://www.economist.com/science-and-technology/2017/12/07/women-ask-fewer-questions-than-men-at-seminars (accessed 13 September 2023).

This intrigues me, and I wanted to find out the impact of this on women in the Church. So, to start my research, I shared the article above on my Facebook page and asked if anyone had experienced this. More than one hundred comments and many private messages came in. The majority said they identified with what I was asking. But one comment stopped me in my tracks: 'Sorry, Nay, but why does it matter if women speak less? Aren't we all according to James 1:19 meant to be quick to listen and slow to speak?'

Why does it matter if women don't speak much? Why does it matter if they speak 80% or 70% less? Ultimately, it matters because God calls men and women to be his representatives, his ambassadors. When women's voices aren't heard, when they aren't living as God's representatives, half of the image of God is not being seen in our world, and half of God's image is being eradicated from the mission of the Church. It is really striking that, despite the cultural context of the New Testament, women were called to use their voices in significant ways – and this is something that is true regardless of where you lie on the complementarian/egalitarian spectrum.

Here are a few examples from the Facebook discussion:

Helen
What I find so interesting about this is that the accepted perception is that women speak *more*. I've wanted to record meetings and count words so I could challenge that stereotype – it is so easily thrown around – to demonstrate that the women present were *not* talking lots more than the guys, in fact.

Mary
I'm a physicist and have similar experiences! You learn to adapt in male-dominated environments. The default is that women's voices and opinions are viewed as less important. Sometimes you must be 'difficult' to be heard. I have seen

and experienced this so many times. Women don't want to be rude and talk over someone else, male or female. Men don't necessarily strive to be rude, but they're used to being listened to. This has led to many conversations where I or another woman in the conversation stop speaking when interrupted. Even if she perseveres to finish her sentence, she doesn't interrupt the person speaking to her.

Most of the stories and responses were heartbreaking. Grown women who were being treated as second class, second rate to men. Throughout my reading and observing, I've found solace in the pages of Scripture. Genesis 1:26–8 is very clear that, from the beginning, the Bible shows that both men and women are valuable, both bear and embody together God's image and, as such, both are God's representatives and ambassadors called to rule over the earth. If we believe the Bible and live committed to God's word, then surely the experience women have in the Church must be different from the testimonies above, right? Let's hear from three women about their experience in church.

Edith
Throughout my life and in church I have learned not to speak when there's a majority of men (especially older men), because I expected either to be ignored, shushed, ridiculed, belittled or aggressively put down. There is a handful of men (less than a handful) who have asked for my opinion, where I didn't feel as if they were waiting for me to finish just to explain to me how wrong I was.

Sally
I was reading up on a heavy topic for a group at theological college. I ended up taking a position that was different from that of everyone else. Now, for twenty-five years, I've kept

silent on my position, except with my children and a few friends recently. In my previous jobs (research physicist, later teacher), I had no problem presenting a different point of view if I was convinced of it, confident that people would listen to me and the argument I put forward on the merit of the case I made. In contrast, I assumed that within church I would suffer a loss of credibility if I made my position known, and that people would mostly dismiss the argument out of hand as 'wrong' before considering the merits of the case. I felt constrained to behave differently in church from out of church. Expecting to be taken seriously and engaged with outside of church, but to be dismissed as 'an easily deceived woman' inside church.

Susan

For women like me who are introverts, and who like to form their thoughts before speaking, it presents an extra challenge if, statistically, we are already less likely to speak in certain situations. And churches that continue to be heavily male-led (with only men in teaching and leadership roles) will already have fewer women involved in their meetings and decision-making, so these women already have an uphill challenge to influence any change or decisions, and then your article highlights even more reasons that make it harder to contribute as women in these scenarios.

As we reflect upon these statistics and testimonies, we need to start asking some hard questions about our practice in the Church, so let's start with the problem.

1 Assess the problem

I asked Edith what would help her to speak, and she said:

I think the first thing is to realise there is a problem. It's so easily dismissed, by both men and women. And it makes it worse for women who want to serve. At least in my case, it creates frustration and bitterness, which is not a good place to be in if you want to serve. I feel there should be regular conversations in the church structures. These should be mediated by both men and women who have expertise in the field of male–female dynamics and gender roles, and who are able to recognise unhealthy patterns of behaviour, both in men and women.

We need to recognise there is a problem, assess it, understand it within our own context and commit to change. Women may be chatty and in the majority in church life, but when it comes to speaking up in Bible study, church meetings or open prayer, many will be unable to do so.

I asked a Facebook group of church leaders to share their experiences on this topic, and here are the responses I received:

As a student, I was told never to pray first in a prayer meeting, as a way of encouraging men to lead. It's become embedded, though, and I never pray first! The implication I took from this is that women weren't to lead anything in the spiritual/Bible sphere.

I grew up in the world of camps (to which I credit with thanks my love of expository Bible teaching). Women were encouraged to teach (young people) but I certainly never (in ten years of camps) heard a woman teach core topics such as the cross. The most pronounced moment was when there became a change in practice for the taskforce/helper team. Suddenly female team members were no longer allowed to be on the rota to lead their team prayer meetings. The reason

I was given was that we have a responsibility to provide a training ground for male leaders. I was hit by the sudden confusion that not only were women not allowed to teach other men or have an overall leadership role, but there could be a whole realm of other areas of basic Christian ministry that we may be steered away from, to enable the training of male leaders.

It's over to you now to assess the problem.

Questions for discussion
- Which of these stories do you identify with?
- Can you recall a time when you didn't feel able to speak?
- What would have helped you in that situation?
- Think back to your last prayer meeting, Bible study, leaders' meeting or Q&A after a talk. Who spoke first?

As friends from around the world and across the Church have read these original blogs, they've been in touch with me. Many of them have discussed and are now discussing how to listen to women on this topic. I was encouraged to receive this from a pastor:

Jim
Thank you, this is a helpful discussion; I'll share it with our staff. Over the past eighteen months, we as a church have gone through a helpful and often challenging process of looking at these issues together. We as elders read *Developing Female Leaders* by Kadi Cole as a starting point and then gathered several groups of women over the past year to listen to women's experiences in our church and consider how we can grow in helping women to flourish.

My hope is that this book can be read and discussed together and become the start of a conversation.

2 Make some simple changes

Address the first question to women

The research shows that the statistics change when a woman goes first. If a woman asks the first question, then men and women both ask around 50% of the questions that follow. On one level, there is a simple answer: make sure that whoever is leading the meeting addresses the first question to a woman. Academic lecturers have taken to directing their first question to a woman and have noticed a difference when they do this. So, next time there is a prayer meeting, you could just simply ask the leader to invite a woman to pray first; it would be even kinder to give the woman concerned some warning.

You might think that what I'm talking about is just poor group dynamics, but it's more than that. Over the next few weeks, take time to assess what happens in your prayer meetings and Bible studies. Who contributes? What do they say? Who doesn't speak? As you notice the disparity, you'll need to intentionally bring more women into leadership.

Sarah shares some thoughts on how to improve female participation:

> One technique that has been shown to increase the numbers of women who ask questions is to give the audience time for a short period of discussion. This gives women (and shy men) confidence that their question is valid and interesting and so leads to higher numbers of questions from women.

Understand that one isn't enough

Women are more likely to speak up if there is more than one woman in the group. I've sat in countless meetings, Bible studies, leadership teams and steering committees where I am the only woman. By simply adding a few more women to these groups, you will notice women contributing more. In 2018, Egon Zehnder, who represented the Global Board Diversity Tracker, said this: 'You need at least three female directors to create a critical mass, this is called the "magic number".' With at least two female colleagues, women are more likely to speak up and be heard.[4]

I once presented some of these statistics to a leadership team. In response, one of the men said, 'Surely this isn't true?' then one of the women cagily raised her hand and said:

> Earlier in our group discussion, I wanted to say something straightaway but just couldn't pluck up the courage. I waited another thirty seconds and thought, 'It's too late now; I can't say anything.' Then two minutes later, still counting, I thought to myself, 'Is it too late to speak after two minutes?' Eventually, after all the internal deliberation, I decided it really was too late to say anything at all.

The room laughed nervously out loud.

3 Value women's voices

In contrast to all I've said above, women in the Bible are often the first to do something significant with their voice. The Gospels present three occasions in which women were proclaimers of Jesus: the Lukan infancy narrative, the story of the Samaritan woman and the accounts of the women at the tomb in the resurrection narratives. This is surprising as, in first-century society, it was seen as inappropriate for women to speak with men who weren't their

---

4 Egon Zehnder, 'Who's Really on Board? Making Diverse Boards More Effective Boards', Global Board Diversity Tracker, 5 November 2021: https://www. egonzehnder.com/global-board-diversity-tracker (accessed 13 September 2023).

husbands, and women rarely spoke in public. Jesus' treatment of women was radically different. Jesus' way was a sign of the new way of living in the kingdom of God that Jesus inaugurated!

Below is a list of places where women's voices are significant. I credit and thank Eric Schumacher[5] for pointing out many of these.

- Hagar is the first and only character to give God a name in the Old Testament. She 'gave this name to the LORD' in Genesis 16:13: 'You are the God who sees me.'
- Hannah, in 1 Samuel 2:10, is the first person to use the term 'anointed one', in a time of terrible corruption where the word of God was rarely heard: 'He will give strength to his king and exalt the horn of his anointed.'
- In Luke 1:38, women are the first to believe that Jesus and John the Baptist would be conceived and the first to speak aloud of it. '"I am the Lord's servant," Mary answered. "May your word to me be fulfilled." Then the angel left her.'
- Elizabeth and her unborn child are the first recorded people to recognise the Messiah's arrival in Luke 1:42: 'In a loud voice she exclaimed: "Blessed are you among women and blessed is the child you will bear!"'
- Elizabeth is the first recorded person to declare the Messiah's presence on earth in Luke 1:43: 'But why am I so favoured, that the mother of my Lord should come to me?'
- Mary speaks the New Testament's first poetic song praising God for the Messiah's arrival in Luke 1:46–7: 'And Mary said: "My soul glorifies the Lord, and my spirit rejoices in God my Saviour."'
- A woman is the first recorded Gentile to recognise Jesus as the Messiah and the first to go and tell a community about him in

5 Eric Schumacher, '21 Places Women Emerge Front and Center in Scripture's Storyline', The Gospel Coalition, 2 June 2018: https://www.thegospelcoalition.org/article/21-places-women-emerge-front-and-center-in-scriptures-storyline (accessed 13 September 2023).

John 4:42. 'They said to the woman, "We no longer believe just because of what you said; now we have heard for ourselves, and we know that this man really is the Saviour of the world."'

- Women were the first tasked with proclaiming the good news of the resurrection in Matthew 28:7: 'Then go quickly and tell his disciples: "He has risen from the dead and is going ahead of you into Galilee. There you will see him." Now I have told you.'

4 Commit to long-term encouragement

Many women need to be encouraged and given the opportunity to use their voices. This needs to be done in the context of friendships, intentional mentoring and lots of support. Sadly this rarely happens to women, though I've repeatedly seen younger men taken under the wing of a pastor or a senior leader – they're often known as 'the blokes worth watching'. A well-respected leader carried around a small booklet in his shirt pocket with the names of forty men he was mentoring. It's wonderful that he invested so much in these men. But what about the women: were they not worth investing in? Or even their wives: were they not worth praying for and asking after? Throughout my thirties, I watched male peers invited to be trained by their churches, sent to theological college and persuaded to stay longer in new roles at work. I need to be honest: my heart sank. I knew this wouldn't happen to me; I had reached a glass ceiling. In writing about this topic, I've discovered that I'm not alone. Here are two case studies:

Laura
The ones to watch, the ones to build up, the ones to give opportunities to: these always seem to be the young men. At first, I thought it was my own heart playing a comparison game. But, when there is a clear pattern of opportunity, you can't help but feel as if there's a special club you are not a

part of. Whether it's giving a young man who can play four chords the chance to lead worship, or when someone studying theology has the chance to speak at an event. When there is a clear pattern of opportunity you can't help but feel like this.

Lisa

I started working in a new context in youth ministry. I looked around at the groups across our region and realised there hadn't been a single female speaker all year. Recently, in a planning weekend, the notion of having a female speaker was mentioned but conversation was shut down immediately. So, I asked the question, 'Are there women who could speak, do you think?' No answer. As I reflected on the women I knew, I realised that very few of them had been given the opportunity even to try. There were some who were given the chance to speak, but sadly their talks weren't perfect. After that point, they were no longer invited; it was as if they'd been blacklisted. In contrast, male friends seemed to be given plentiful opportunities. If they messed up, then the response was, 'No worries, we'll invite them back.' I try to be gracious as I look on and cheer on my brothers in Christ. But I can't help wondering if anyone asks where the women are. No wonder we are so afraid to fail.

Surely the metaphor of men and women working together as a body leaves no space for us to say to each other, 'I don't need you.' What do Lisa and Laura need?

Let's turn to Philippians and see a vision of encouragement, friendship and partnership in the gospel. This letter shows us Paul's theology of friendship. Despite not mentioning the word, Paul uses the terms fellowship, partnership (Philippians 1:5, 7; 3:10; 4:14, 15), like-mindedness and understanding or care (Philippians 1:7; 2:2, 5; 3:15; 4:2, 10). Two characteristics appear in Paul's theology of friendship:

The first is the giving and receiving of gifts (immaterial and material) between Paul and the Philippians. This stems from a mutual way of thinking, feeling, and acting patterned after Jesus Christ (Philippians 2:5–11). The second characteristic in Paul's ideal definition of friendship is enduring suffering on behalf of the other.[6]

A quick read of Philippians 1 shows the extent of suffering that Paul endured on behalf of the Philippians. This book overflows with fellowship, partnership, friendship, like-mindedness, understanding and care. We're made for friendship, but we seem to struggle with the idea of this friendship being between men and women. Philippians points to the closeness of Paul and these women (Philippians 1:5, 12, 14): they've contended with him, and they've furthered the spread of the gospel together. As you read, you can hear the closeness that Paul has with them: a commitment to them as individuals, as co-workers and as friends.

But what could this look like? Here are some stories from where women have been intentionally encouraged by men in their lives.

Alison

My work retreat days have been a refuge for the past six years. These days are made by people, and it has been a deep privilege to be shaped by and to shape others within these teams, past and present. I listened to a podcast recently where it was said that gospel culture is a friendship-rich environment. There are no better words to embody how I feel about these brothers and sisters. Having men on the team to cheer me on and champion me has been a wonderful experience and one I don't take for granted.

---

6 David E. Briones, 'Paul's Theology of Friendship', Westminster Theological Seminary, 21 October 2019: https://faculty.wts.edu/posts/pauls-theology-of-friendship (accessed 13 September 2023).

Nay

Twenty years ago, I did a volunteer year. We were put into small groups of four: two men and two women. Through this, I met Kenny. He is a long-term friend who texts and phones regularly. He checks in to see how I am; he and his wife pray for me and support me, but he's the one who does the checking in with me. I can't think of anyone else who has shown me more clearly what a brother in Christ looks like, because he's not afraid to be my friend.

Malcolm was a part of my church. He prayed for me and took an interest in what I wrote on my blogs; he bought me books and spoke up on my behalf. Sadly, Mary, his wife, died a few years ago. Up until then, they would encourage and disciple younger men and women in the church together. For years, many Iranian men and women were supported by them. When Mary died, Malcolm began to question whether he should continue interacting with women in this way, or whether it would be inappropriate. Malcolm continued to love, support and encourage women because he knew how valuable they were to God. At his funeral, it was the testimony of young women that struck me the most.

Questions for discussion

- There are many places in the Bible where women use their voices for the first time and in a significant way. Which of the women's voices surprises you the most?
- How could women's voices be encouraged more in your church?
- What are the reasons why this doesn't happen?
- Whom could you commit to encouraging?

She needs brothers

Only 41% of people in Germany said they felt very comfortable with a woman being the head of government.[1]

Just then his disciples returned and were surprised to find him talking with a woman.
(John 4:27)

A BBC article entitled, 'Why Do We Still Distrust Women Leaders?' caught my attention: despite Angela Merkel's long-time chancellorship, 41% of people in Germany felt very uncomfortable with a woman being the head of a government.[2] Despite many advances for women in leadership, there are still some deep-seated cultural biases that are hard to shift. One thing for sure is that it isn't about competence. The Harvard Business Review discussed findings from their analysis of 360-degree employee reviews.[3] They found that women in leadership positions were perceived as being every bit as effective as men. Women excelled in taking the initiative, acting with resilience, practising self-development, driving for results, and displaying high integrity and honesty. Yet their data shows that, when women assess themselves, they are not as generous in their ratings.

Is it possible that we mistrust people in their role because they are women? Is it possible that, despite their competence, women

1   Christine Ro, 'Why Do We Still Distrust Women Leaders?' BBC Worklife, 19 January 2021: https://www.bbc.com/worklife/article/20210108-why-do-we-still-distrust-women-leaders (accessed 13 September 2023).

2   Ro, 'Why Do We Still Distrust Women Leaders?'

3   Jack Zenger and Joseph Folkman, 'Research: Women Score Higher Than Men in Most Leadership Skills', 25 June 2019: https://hbr.org/2019/06/research-women-score-higher-than-men-in-most-leadership-skills (accessed 13 September 2023).

even mistrust themselves? I'm interested in how this applies in the Church and, if it does apply, how it presents itself.

How do men and women relate in the Church?

How men and women relate to each other matters, because the good news of Jesus is all about relationships. How we relate to one another says something about what we understand and believe about God himself. The gospel message can only be shown as we relate to others, because repentance, forgiveness and restoration can't be done as individuals. At the very heart of the Church, there is such potential for men and women to work together, and yet the reality we see in the Church today is so broken and so flawed. I asked a few friends what they thought of the BBC quote and what their experience was. Here's what they shared with me:

Maria
I was appointed in my new role as Director of a Christian charity. Afterwards, I was informed that some of the senior leaders had abstained from voting because I am a woman. They commented: 'A woman could not be as spiritually insightful as a man; a woman cannot hear from God in the same way as men can.'

Hannah
I was about to finish my job and a friend said to me, 'I really hope you are replaced with a man.' I was left shocked. I don't think she really thought about what she was saying to me; there was no qualification or explanation. It hurt.

Maybe you haven't had anything said to you so bluntly or clearly, maybe it's been more subtle. I often get questioned about why I discuss these topics of women and the Church on social media.

Many metaphors have been used to describe me: 'Don't drag others through the mud', 'Don't go fishing for problems', 'Stop washing the Church's dirty laundry in public'. And yet some people, mostly women, write to me and thank me for speaking into these situations. How women are treated by others is a really important issue, both for those who are Christians and for the watching world. I find that, whenever I write about these issues, friends read my posts, and then on the way home from the school run or during a swim I often get asked questions. Inevitably, it ends up with me saying, 'This is not how Jesus regards women; read the Gospels and you'll see something radical and so very different.'

Jen Wilkin helpfully describes some of these broken relationships and suspicions. She calls them the three female ghosts that haunt the Church. In her article of the same name, she identifies them as the Child, the Usurper and the Temptress. She says:

> These three ghosts glide into staff meetings where key decisions are made. They hover in classrooms where theology is taught. They linger in prayer rooms where the weakest among us give voice to hurt. They strike fear into the hearts of both men and women, and worse, they breathe fear into the interactions between them. Their every intent is to cripple the ability of men and women to minister to and with one another.[4]

I was aware of some of these ghosts in my own life, but I wanted to find out if friends had experienced them too.

The Child

Many years ago, I was at a conference. I tried to join a conversation with two male acquaintances, but their response was, 'Go away, silly

---

4 Jen Wilkin, '3 Female Ghosts That Haunt the Church', The Gospel Coalition, 12 February 2015: https://www.thegospelcoalition.org/article/3-female-ghosts-that-haunt-the-church (accessed 13 September 2023).

little girl.' I felt sick and stupid, and just wished I could disappear. Women are often treated as children; decisions are made for them, and they are patronised and humiliated in conversations.

Here are three examples from friends

Danielle

Being a young leader in a charity and at the same time a woman is really challenging. Some of the difficulties I face involve my work alongside pastors in the Church. Because I am a woman, they don't pay much attention to the work I do, or to my invitation to partner. The fact that I am young puts even greater pressure on me. In my country, a young woman leading an organisation doesn't sound like something serious. I have had so many situations where my husband was heard and listened to, even though he was saying the same thing as I was. The other challenge for me is how the younger men perceive me; they are often reserved when talking or discussing different topics with me. There is that invisible fight for the right to be right because they are male and I am a woman. Even though I might be older or more experienced.

Esther

I was invited to present my work at a pastors' meeting because the 'leader' had met my father and liked him. The guy introduced me, mentioning he had met my father and that he was a great guy. I was 36 or 37 at the time and had been attending those meetings for six years. I wasn't aware that I needed my dad's name to develop my own ministry.

Caroline

I was excited for the new vicar to join us at the church where I was working as a youth leader. I was anxious to get to know him and everything seemed fine for a while, but soon that changed. He didn't make much effort to get to know me; we didn't have regular meetings and he never gave me any idea of what he was expecting of me, so I bumbled along as best I could. There were a few times when he let the church wardens shout at me and send me abusive emails, and he always took their side. I was meeting up with an older woman in the church and, one morning, instead of meeting at my house, she asked me to come to the church with her. I went in and there was the vicar. I had no idea what he wanted. He sat me down and told me he wanted me to leave. He told me people were complaining about me, and parents were unhappy with me. He provided no evidence of this, nor could he name one person who had said this. Instead, he treated me like a child.

Each of these women were treated by others as a child. I wonder if any aspects of these stories resonate with you?

Here are some clues that you might be being treated as a Child
- Others are making decisions for you.
- You have been patronised or humiliated in front of others.
- Others are controlling you.
- Your independence is discouraged.
- You are told what to do in your free time.
- Male peers are given more freedom than you.

We'll look later at what Danielle, Esther and Caroline need and how Jesus' words could be used to respond to the ghost of the Child.

The Usurper
This is the one that, in the long dark corridors of the night, I bump into the most. I was at a conference and noticed a pattern emerging. I asked a friend why he thought that other men didn't

seem to want to sit with me at mealtimes or hang out at break times. He replied, 'Sometimes men see women like you as a threat.' At another conference, I enquired why the steering committee was all male and I asked if they would consider including a woman in this group. The response was, 'Nay, that is one step too far ... If we invited a woman on to the steering committee, it would cause such disunity that the conference would split.' And yet the conference was for men and women. For me, this wasn't just a tick-box exercise; I wasn't trying to be troublesome: to me this really mattered. Having women on the team would have made a huge difference to the culture and atmosphere of the conference. At a minimum, it would have meant that the conference was designed with women in mind. But if you value and support women's voices being heard, then having just one woman on the planning team can lead to an 18% higher proportion of invited female speakers. This statistic is taken from research about academic conferences and the impact that having a diverse conference planning team makes.[5]

Here are three examples from friends

Kathy

I've found the reaction and response to my own call to leadership very interesting. The model of married ministry for women feels so hard ... It seems to be 'OK' if your husband is also a senior leader in ministry, but not if he's in secular work. I'm grateful that I'm now on the discernment pathway for Anglican ordained ministry. We've been struck by how many reactions have been explicitly or implicitly challenging, because I am the one following that call, not

---

5 Arturo Casadevall and Jo Handelsman, 'The Presence of Female Conveners Correlates with a Higher Proportion of Female Speakers at Scientific Symposia', National Library of Medicine, 7 January 2014: https://www.ncbi.nlm.nih.gov/pmc/articles/PMC3884059 (accessed 14 September 2023).

my husband. He continues to support my call 100% but he doesn't share it. Comments have ranged from suggesting I am selfish (not putting my family and kids first), to saying I am inappropriately dominant (spiritually or just in our marriage) or just naive (clearly not realising the impact this will have on my poor husband).

Susie

I worked in a charity as a manager. One of my supervisees made it clear that he didn't want to be managed by a woman. When I left my job, it was said that this was because we had a character clash, and that this supervisee should not have a female supervisor.

Katie

I noticed how people reacted when I left my job and was replaced by a man. I heard this response a few times: how good it was that there was a man taking over the job. This left me with the impression that I had taken a man's job.

Here are some clues that you might be being treated as a Usurper

- Your character is questioned.
- You're told you have ideas above your station.
- Your ideas are treated with suspicion.
- Your suggestions for change are treated with defensiveness.
- Others think you want their job.
- People admit they're afraid of you.
- Men don't talk to you at conferences or at church.
- You feel unsure that what you have experienced is real.
- It's implied that anything other than being a wife and mother is a failure.
- You're told you should be replaced by a man.

- You're accused of disunity.
- Your husband is accused of being weak.

What do Kathy, Susie and Katie need? We'll see below how Jesus interacts with a Usurper.

The Temptress

I've not struggled with this one, or at least I don't know that I've struggled with it! Others too found it hard to think of examples. My friend Lizzie commented, 'This one, out of all of them, is the one you're not going to know about. This is the one that will most likely be said about you behind your back or in the absence of company.'

Here are two examples from friends

Sam

My god-kids' dad and I are good friends. We often drive home together, or I stay over at their house. We chat in the kitchen, all together as a family, in our pyjamas. When I've shared this with others, so many people have said this to me: 'Don't you think it's inappropriate that you stayed over, that you spent time in a car together? What does that look like?' It seems that we can't have a brother/sister relationship without people commenting. When they had a new-born, I helped. I took the kids and went with Rob to a local park, so that his wife could sleep at home. Even then, friends commented: 'Are you sure you should be doing this? Aren't you getting between a husband and his wife and his new-born baby?' If I spend time with his wife, no one complains, and yet she feels as much a sister as he is a brother.

Ellie

I was told that I needed to dress in such a way that it didn't reveal anything that might 'cause a brother to stumble'. It was only in my late twenties when I started hearing the flipside of this: that we should be holding men to account for their own thoughts. I hadn't realised that I'm not responsible for someone else's thoughts; they are. I think we should credit men with more self-control and allow a positive expectation to produce a positive result.

Here are some clues that you might be being treated as a Temptress

- Men (and some women) can't look you in the eye.
- At conferences, people choose to sit with other men rather than with you.
- People don't see you as a friend.
- Your choice of clothes is questioned.
- Socialising doesn't happen, just work or ministry.
- Within the first sentence, women talk about their husband, or men about their wives.

For many, these comments have become so normalised that we can't see the implications. If we do, we fear talking about it for the backlash that we'll face. Sometimes others will clearly disagree, other times it is more subtle, sometimes it comes in a form of surprise or a look.

What do Sam and Ellie need? We'll see below how Jesus interacts with a Temptress.

A question for discussion
Which of these ghosts do you and your friends most identify with?

A vision for the Church

We've seen, in earlier chapters, the beautiful vision for the Church as one body. A body where we can use our gifts, seeing them as essential to the functioning of the body. But how do we do this when there are such barriers between how men and women relate? What could it look like in practice? First, we need to stop viewing women as Children, Usurpers or Temptresses. Instead, let's see them as sisters, disciples and co-workers. Jen Wilkin says, 'In the un-haunted church where love trumps fear, women are viewed (and view themselves) as allies rather than antagonists, sisters rather than seductresses, co-laborers rather than children.'[6] Let's look at how Jesus responds to these three suspicions.

Co-labourers not children

Jesus does not treat women in a patronising, derogatory way. He treats them with dignity and gives them key roles in the story of redemptive history. In Luke 24:11, the disciples 'did not believe the women, because their words seemed to them like nonsense'. Yet, there seem to be many places where women are key eyewitnesses to Jesus' birth, death and resurrection. At the end of John's Gospel, we see that Mary Magdalene was the first eyewitness to the empty tomb. John 20:1 says, 'Early on the first day of the week, while it was still dark, Mary Magdalene went to the tomb and saw that the stone had been removed from the entrance.' Who was Mary Magdalene? Tim Keller says this about her:

> There is a very, very long tradition, a very early and strong tradition, in the Western Christian church especially (and in the Eastern church) that Mary Magdalene was a prostitute in Magdala, which would have certainly fit in. In fact, it wouldn't have been a compliment to call somebody a Magdalene. All we know for sure is Mary Magdalene came from an incredibly broken background. Her life was a wreck.

---

6 Wilkin, '3 Female Ghosts That Haunt the Church'.

She was a broken person, and Jesus had put her back together.[7]

In Luke 8, we see Jesus casting out demons from Mary and then witness the transformation as this same woman becomes one of Jesus' travelling companions, a part of his ministry team. In these same verses, you'll see that it was the women who provided out of their own means (Luke 8:3).

Disciples not usurpers

In the first century, women were effectively banned from public life and spent most of their time serving as wives, servants and mothers. Men and women didn't talk in public and women wouldn't have learnt alongside men. Into this context, we see Jesus living in a radically different way from other men around him. Let's look at Mary: she could have been treated as a usurper but, instead, Jesus saw her as a disciple.

As Jesus and his disciples were on their way, he came to a village where a woman named Martha opened her home to him. She had a sister called Mary, who sat at the Lord's feet listening to what he said. But Martha was distracted by all the preparations that had to be made. She came to him and asked, 'Lord, don't you care that my sister has left me to do the work by myself? Tell her to help me!'

'Martha, Martha,' the Lord answered, 'you are worried and upset about many things, but few things are needed – or indeed only one. Mary has chosen what is better, and it will not be taken away from her.'
(Luke 10:38–42)

---

7 Tim Keller, 'Mary Meets Jesus', Gospel in Life podcast, 15 April 2020: https://podcast.gospelinlife.com/e/mary-meets-jesus (accessed 14 September 2023).

See how Mary was commended for being a disciple: she sat at Jesus' feet and listened to his teaching. Martha, rather surprisingly, was criticised for serving and offering hospitality. This is such a counter-cultural situation, and yet Jesus is commending Mary for having chosen the better way.

There are some culturally unusual things here. First, that women were even viewed as disciples at all. In the first century, women would not have been allowed to learn, and yet Jesus invited the sisters to do exactly that. Second, the disciples would have chosen their rabbi, not the other way round. Here, Jesus the rabbi chose Mary to be his disciple; this would have been outrageous to others, but what an affirmation to Mary, that she too was called to go and make disciples in his name. Third, when the culture was screaming that women should be in the kitchen preparing food for their guests, Jesus did the opposite: he invited Martha to stop worrying and working and instead to listen and learn from him. Mary chose to sit and listen to Jesus, whereas Martha was still serving. Martha was thinking that Jesus wanted her service rather than her ears and her heart.

Despite Jesus appointing and investing in female disciples, many still question how sensible this is. Can men and women be disciples together? Can they sit and learn together at conferences or in church? Our discipleship seems so monochrome. I often see photos of male friends at leadership conferences: they're learning together, discussing with and inspiring one another, and often there's not a woman in sight. Imagine, instead, if women were treated as co-workers and had opportunities to grow and serve according to their gifts. Imagine churches overflowing with men and women learning and building up the Church together. As you look at your church, is there room for an educated laywoman such as Priscilla, an adventurous pioneer such as Phoebe or a granny such as Timothy's? The Bible commends breadth in the Church. Galatians 3:28 says, 'There is neither Jew nor Gentile, neither slave nor free, nor is there male and female, for you are all one in Christ Jesus.'

Sisters not temptresses

In John 4, Jesus' disciples were surprised to find him talking with a woman at a well. This was a Samaritan woman, and a woman with a questionable marital history. Of all people she could have been viewed as a temptress, but not by Jesus.

> Just then his disciples returned and were surprised to find him talking with a woman. But no one asked, 'What do you want?' or 'Why are you talking with her?'
>
> Then, leaving her water jar, the woman went back to the town and said to the people, 'Come, see a man who told me everything I've ever done. Could this be the Messiah?' They came out of the town and made their way toward him ...
>
> Many of the Samaritans from that town believed in him because of the woman's testimony, 'He told me everything I've ever done.' So, when the Samaritans came to him, they urged him to stay with them, and he stayed two days. And because of his words many more became believers.
> (John 4:27–30, 39–41)

Jesus bucks cultural norms; he treats women with dignity and validates them as human beings made in the image of God. Not only is he willing to spend time with the Samaritan woman, despite racial tensions between Jews and Samaritans, but he sits down, listens to her and talks theology with her. I love this story and the transformation that happened because of her encounter with Jesus. She was the first recorded Gentile to recognise Jesus as the Messiah, and she was the first to go and tell a community about him. For me, her story is a compelling reason in favour of women being evangelists, women communicating the good news of Jesus Christ. As she spoke, many came to believe in Jesus for themselves. In this passage, it's not the temptress who causes shock and surprise, it's Jesus and the way he values women.

After two decades of working in ministry, I have very few close friends. I think one of the reasons is because I'm a woman and I've worked in mostly male environments. Men don't see me as a friend. In all that time, there has only been one colleague who became a friend. He keeps in touch, phones me for a catch-up and is happy to support me and pray for me.

Imagine if, instead of adopting the model of these three ghosts, we treated one another differently? If we treated one another in all purity as brothers and sisters. Aimee Byrd says: 'We have lost the beauty of brotherhood and sisterhood – distinction between the sexes that doesn't reduce them to sex alone. The way we relate to one another sends a message – to one another and to the watching world.'[8]

Questions for discussion

- Can you see the breadth that the Bible commends in how to disciple young leaders?
- What change would happen if women were viewed as disciples, sisters and co-workers?

---

8 Aimee Byrd, *Why Can't We Be Friends? Avoidance is not purity* (Phillipsburg, NJ: P&R Publishing, 2018), Kindle edn, Introduction.

She needs you to stop fudging the issue

Employees who experience role clarity are 53% more efficient and 27% more effective at work than employees who have role ambiguity.[1]

From him the whole body, joined and held together by every supporting ligament, grows and builds itself up in love, as each part does its work.
(Ephesians 4:16)

Recent research shows that clarity in the workplace is essential for workers and, as I've read and thought, I've been wondering if the same is true for the role of women in the Church. For decades, I've seen women sent by their church to work abroad, where they end up leading, pioneering and teaching in churches. Yet, when back at their home church, they are barely allowed to do more than give an interview. Am I alone in observing this and wondering what is going on?

Maybe you've experienced this yourself? Within one setting, you're free to lead and yet, in another, these opportunities don't present themselves or aren't allowed. Or perhaps you're invited to teach at the church plant but not at the main church. Or maybe there's inconsistency in another area.

In this chapter, we aren't going to look at specifics such as how much women are asked to do when they're home on

---

1 Lieke Pijnacker, 'HR Analytics: Role Clarity Impacts Performance', Effectory, 25 September 2019: https://www.effectory.com/knowledge/hr-analytics-role-clarity-impacts-performance (accessed 14 September 2023).

furlough, nor will I address specific theological positions on women in ministry. For the latter, I have some great reading recommendations at the end of the book. What I'm questioning here is inconsistency within our own theological framework. I've worked for two decades in a charity that, at its heart, celebrates unity among a diversity of Evangelical churches. Through my engagement and writing, I genuinely want to honour and respect different viewpoints on the role of women in the Church. But, while respecting the contours of differing theological frameworks and viewpoints, I want to question some common inconsistencies regarding the role of women in church and I want to communicate what that can feel like.

Theological inconsistency and calling

Here are a few examples of inconsistency in women's roles within the Church, taken from the experiences of friends:

Sally
I was encouraged by my church to take part in a summer team event abroad. I was involved in giving an evangelistic talk there, yet when I returned home, I wasn't even allowed to give a report in the church service. A male youth leader read it on my behalf.

Rosie
I'm financially supported by my church to help church-plant in Europe. As part of this, I lead, teach and train others, but back in my sending church this simply wouldn't be allowed.

Hannah
My church regularly invites me to speak at the plant church, but they haven't once invited me to speak at the main church.

Let's go back in history to find some help, as inconsistency isn't a new problem. By 1900, there were two missionary women in China for every male missionary. These Western women found themselves gifted for work in teaching and evangelism in ways that would have been impossible in their churches at home.

Valerie Griffiths writes soberingly:

> In the 1900s if the call of God came to women in Britain, it had to be lived out in a Western culture cluttered with centuries of history and traditions that sometimes had little to do with the Christian faith but constrained them as Christian women. In China away from all that, they were set free to take up opportunities of service unknown in most of their home churches today.[2]

So, the problem isn't new, it's been around for a while. Because women couldn't serve in churches, they went overseas.

If women can't serve in their home church, then let them serve abroad; this was the ethos of church leaders and missionaries from the 1800s onwards. I'm sure the Church outside of the UK has benefited from many gifted and godly women. But, for me, there are many problems with this. This culturally bound perspective jars with that of the New Testament. I originally posted this chapter as a blog. Eddie Arthur tweeted a response and said, 'This says so much about how we view both women and Christians outside of the West.'[3] But, to keep focused, I want to concentrate on the impact inconsistency has on women in the Church. How does this inconsistency and lack of clarity affect women? What do women

---

2 Valerie Griffiths, *Not Less Than Everything: The courageous women who carried the Christian gospel to China* (Oxford: Monarch Books/Overseas Missionary Fellowship, 2004), p. 32.

3 Eddie Arthur, Twitter, 5 November 2021.

like Sally, Rosie and Hannah need? First, we need to find out how it affects them.

How inconsistency makes women feel

Here is what the three friends quoted above have said about this lack of clarity and its impact on them:

Sally
It's extremely demoralising for a teenager. I'm sure it's even more frustrating for grown women who only want to tell everyone about the work they are doing for God.

Rosie
I've seen this a lot and have been really confused by it. If a church holds the view that it is not for women to lead, and if they stand by this in their church in the UK, why is it OK for them to send a woman out to lead a church often in a less affluent and more dangerous part of the world? It leads me to wonder if there is a very concerning view that people of other countries and cultures are 'less than' adult men and women in the West, and that therefore it's OK for a woman to teach them.

Hannah
When a church is inconsistent, I find it frustrating. It can leave women in a position where they have uncertainty about what they are 'allowed' to do in a church, meaning that they won't volunteer for fear of being met with suspicion because what they have volunteered for turns out not to be for women.

So, this lack of clarity, contrasted with the impression of being generous, is a big problem. Sitting on the fence about the role of women in the Church may appear generous, but from the ground it is demoralising, frustrating and confusing.

A question for discussion

What about you: what is your experience of theological inconsistency? What is the impact of this inconsistency?

Theological inconsistency and calling

When there is a lack of clarity, it's hard for women to have their calling affirmed. Here are two stories which contrast what it is like for men and women:

A male friend, Sam

At the age of 15, I became a Christian; I was part of an active youth group and was encouraged to speak and to lead. Every time I went to a conference, I had a sense that I really wanted to serve in the ministry, that I really wanted to do ministry. At the same time, my elders took me aside and said I should be considering some kind of full-time ministry; they asked if I would do a year's apprenticeship with them. There was something in my bones; there was no big sign, there was just … something. I just loved the idea of being involved in ministry.

Helen

I grew up in a Christian family and committed to follow Jesus at the early age of 8. My enthusiasm, boldness and leadership skills were commented upon by those around me. At the time I chose to follow Jesus, I felt a strong calling to be a missionary. I was young but determined to live that out as a present calling rather than to wait to see it come to fruition. In my teenage years, I began to question how much I could live out this calling. It seemed that there were some things that only men could do. The guidelines for what a woman could or could not do were either blurry or unspoken.

It came to a peak when I was 16 and at a big Christian summer festival. It was the second year in a row that I had attended and participated in a seminar track on leadership. I had felt a strong call to be a leader but didn't know what to do with it. At one session, there was a time for prayer response for people who felt called to be church leaders. I look back on this and wonder why on earth I went up for prayer. I felt prompted to do so, but what happened next makes me wish that I had never moved from my seat. I went up for prayer and a man told me, 'I'm sorry, but we don't believe that women can be church leaders, and so we cannot pray this for you.' I wasn't the only girl who had gone up to the front for prayer – there were three of us. We were told to pray for one another, that God might show us how to serve him and use our gifts of leadership in other ways. I felt so confused and hurt – I had felt a prompting from the Holy Spirit, or at least I thought I had. And yet, here I was feeling called to something labelled 'impossible', 'unbiblical' and 'ungodly'. What a weird situation to be in as a 16-year-old! I didn't know what to do, so I suppressed any sense of this calling and pretended that it had never happened. I must have misheard God's voice and prompting; I must have misheard any calling to be a leader.

During my time at university, I was a student leader in my Christian Union. I experienced an equality of male and female leadership. We were co-workers together, serving Christ and building his Church through mission and discipleship. There were no different expectations for a man and a woman – we were the same, we were equal. I felt valued, honoured and equipped – able to lead in different areas and considered the same as a man. There was no difference between us. We were both disciples, we were both children of God, we were both servants in his kingdom and we were both called to serve in his mission.

This experience was liberating but it added to my confusion about the role of women in the Church. I had found a place where I felt free to serve and use my gifts, and yet only for a temporary period. It almost felt like a harsh trick. As soon as I finished university, I had to step back into being limited again to the rules of what was allowed in the Church. I asked myself: which experience reflects the role of men and women in God's kingdom? Which one is how it is meant to be?

There is so much uncertainty and difficulty in the way of women figuring out their calling and their role in God's kingdom. It isn't clear, and nobody seems to want to give any definitive answers. We all dance around the issue, thinking that avoidance will help. It doesn't help – lack of clarity undermines women even more. I wish I didn't have this confusion – I wish I could just follow the calling that God has given me to do. But it isn't that simple ... Why did God make it this way? Why did God create me as a woman? Some days, I wish I were a man.

There seems to be a big difference between how men and women are called in the Church. Cynthia Westfall describes it well:

A man's personal call to the ministry is treated with due respect and seriousness in seminaries. There is a reluctance to question or contradict a man's sense of his own call, even if he appears to lack gifts and social skills deemed appropriate for ministry. When a man negotiates his call to ministry, he utilises emotions and experience in accordance with his faith and the grace that he is given. However, the role of variety and experience in the realisation of calling is either explicitly or effectively discounted for women. When a woman determines her call by the same model, using the same criteria, if she comes to the same conclusion as men, she is told her navigational system is broken. A woman is often told that it is invalid for her to utilise her experience and emotions in discovering her call, since she may come up with the wrong conclusion.[4]

Cynthia goes on to note that this way of being called is particularly ironic. First, because women often learn this language from male pastors as they talk about their call. And second, because the procedure and criteria appear to reflect a biblical understanding of gifting, calling and service derived from Romans 12:1–8.

Getting clear

Kadi Cole has written a book called *Developing Female Leaders*. She says that the most important thing you can do as a leader is to get clear on what you believe. She talks about the gap of untapped potential. To discover this, you need to do some reflecting. Have a look at Figure 2. First, there is the line of what you think theologically. Under that is the line of what women think they should be doing, and under that is the line of what women are comfortable doing. Kadi talks about the importance of being clear both in your theology and in aligning your practice with your theology. The figure is taken from Kadi Cole's book and is very useful.[5]

---

4 Cynthia L. Westfall, *Paul and Gender: Reclaiming the Apostle's vision for men and women in Christ* (Grand Rapids, MI: Baker Academic, 2016), p. 213.

5 Kadi Cole, *Developing Female Leaders: Navigate the minefields and release the potential of women in your church* (Nashville, TN: Thomas Nelson, 2019), p. 18.

She needs you to stop fudging the issue

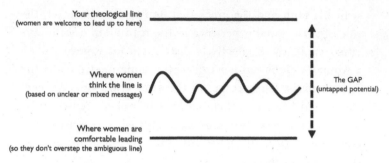

Figure 2 **Being clear in theology and practice**

Questions for discussion

Looking at the table opposite, consider these questions:

- Where is there inconsistency in your examples?
- What lies behind this inconsistency?
- What are the short-term and long-term changes that could be made?
- What surprises you?

This topic can be painful, demoralising, frustrating and confusing. For centuries, we've sent women to make disciples across the world but, for some reason, doing that on our own doorstep is not allowed. Cynthia Westfall says,

The broad spectrum of opinion concerning what exactly is prohibited in what context contributes to the confusion, both for women who are trying to navigate their call and for the churches, organisations and individuals who are trying to apply the prohibition.[6]

---

6   Westfall, *Paul and Gender*, p. 282.

Untapped potential or a gift you would like to explore using	Your church's theological line	Where are these gifts currently used in the church?	Where do you feel comfy leading?	Where is there untapped potential in your gifts?	What is holding you back?
Teaching the Bible	You can teach kids and youth in home group	Kids, youth	Kids, youth and women	I'd like to lead a small group. I would love to teach women.	I feel too nervous. There are no opportunities.

Table 1 **The gap of untapped potential**

If you're in this place, I urge you to take a while to consider Ephesians 4:1–16. You may need to hear again the call to 'bear with one another in love' (v. 2) or the challenge to 'make every effort to keep the unity of the Spirit through the bond of peace' (v. 3), or maybe you need to be reminded that it is 'Christ [who] gave gifts to his people' (v. 7) or that the vision of the body includes 'each part doing its work' (v. 16). This section of Ephesians gives hope that 'speaking the truth in love, we will grow to become in every aspect the mature body of him who is the head, that is, Christ' (v. 15).

What do Sally, Rosie, Hannah and Helen need? They, and we, need church leaders and women to sit down together and talk about this. We need to take time to evaluate inconsistency. Women need to be heard, to share how it makes them feel and work together to find ways for them to use the gifts God has given them.

She needs you to fix the leaky pipe

6,300 Professors in the UK are women – from 23% to 28% of these are in senior posts. This is despite women representing 46% of all academic staff.[1]

So in Christ Jesus you are all children of God through faith. (Galatians 3:26)

I first came across some of these statistics when my husband started working on the Athena Swan committee, which looks at representation of women in Science, Technology, Engineering and Mathematics (STEM). The big questions in science are: where do the women go? And how do we keep women in academia? The statistics are even more shocking when the majority of PhD students are female. Figure 3, from a diagram by Kathleen Grogan,[2] shows many reasons why women disappear.

This research got me thinking about my own experience. I did student work for more than two decades, and I love encouraging people to use their gifts and talents. I've always shown an interest in what people go on to do afterwards and keep in touch with many with whom I've worked. Up until ten years ago, when women finished student work some would return to secular work, some

1 Sean Coughlan, 'Only 1% of UK University Professors Are Black', BBC, 19 January 2021: https://www.bbc.co.uk/news/education-55723120 (accessed 14 September 2023).

2 Kathleen E. Grogan, 'How the Entire Scientific Community Can Confront Gender Bias in the Workplace', Nature Ecology & Evolution, 26 November 2018, Springer Nature: https://www.nature.com/articles/s41559-018-0747-4 (accessed 14 September 2023).

Women are less likely to be employed as graduate students or postdocs in male PIs' labs, which represent over 70% of labs

Women are half as likely to get 'excellent' letters of recommendation and 10–20% less likely to become an independent PI* than men

Start-up funds for male PIs are over US$500,000 more than start-ups for female PIs

Women submit fewer grants overall, fewer renewal or simultaneous grants and are less likely to have renewals funded than men

Female authors are 6.4% less likely to have their manuscripts accepted by an all-male panel of reviewers

Women account for fewer than 25% of awardees for the most prominent awards in some STEM fields

How can the entire STEM community address this gender bias problem?

- Collect and publish data on gender representation in all areas of STEM visibility and success
- Set clear and specific goals and guidelines for gender and minority representation in your area of STEM
- Identify and offer effective training in unconscious bias and effective hiring and retention strategies

*PI in this context in the US means Principal Investigator or Head of Laboratory.

Figure 3 The representation of women in STEM

would start work with a world mission agency, while others became stay-at-home mums. But in the past ten years, this has changed. More women want to return to work after having children and many want to stay working in Christian ministry within the UK. There are many women gifted and trained in ministry seeking opportunities. Yet there seem to be very few options for women. All this has caused me to question: is there a leaky pipe in the Church for women? Is there a leaky pipe for women in paid gospel ministry?

In many churches, a lack of role models and clear pathways for women is a real problem. I've worked for decades with gifted women, but now so many of them have found that certain gifts are shelved and forgotten. For many men and women, their initial experience of paid ministry is life-giving. For men, there is often clear direction beyond this time. Student work or theological college is like a stepping stone to future ministry. For women it's a different story. Beyond these early years of ministry many find themselves with early retirement at the age of 28. Here's what one friend said recently:

> For years, 'ministry trainees' are often used as an excuse to milk energy and optimism from gifted young folks for peanuts. This alone puts many off … but, for many women, the term ministry trainee … is a complete misnomer. The number of female peers I've seen 'trained', only to realise they weren't being trained for anything, is huge. They weren't being trained at all. They were just cheaper than hiring a women's worker.

Of course, many will choose to use their gifts in an unpaid capacity, some will use their gifts in secular work, but some are called to give most of their time to working for their church, Bible college or a para-church organisation. Whatever your situation, I hope there is something here to encourage you. For women, this leaky pipe means that they must shelve some of their gifts. If they can't use them in their church, then the following can happen:

- they can get rusty;
- they think that someone else can do it better than they can;
- they begin to question whether those gifts are for them.

My intention with this book is to help us identify and become aware of our blind spots. As we think about the leaky pipe, we've got the opportunity to start exploring how to help men and women work together and build up the Church as a body. But first, let's consider five ways in which the leadership training pipe is currently leaking talented servants of the gospel – who happen to be women.

Five leaks in the Church

Leak 1 Apprenticeships that lead nowhere

Rachel

I was in a Ministry Apprentice Scheme (MAS) for two years in a church. I completed a ministry training course alongside this. I learnt so much and loved studying the Bible in a deeper way. I grew in my love and in my confidence to give talks, particularly to children. I focused more on children's ministry as my time went on, and found my 'place' in that specific context. As the two years ended, I did what I had already planned and applied to do teacher training. When one of my church leaders asked me, 'But did you consider going into full-time ministry?' I said, 'Yes, of course. Yet no one has ever had a serious conversation with me about it. I am unsure of the kind of "role" I could fulfil in ministry full time while also paying the bills. I don't feel experienced (or qualified!) enough to be a children's worker, and there aren't any obvious local opportunities that fit my giftings.' The leader to whom I said this was very respectful and pastoral and recognised my dilemma. He made a point to learn from the error of not supporting female ministry trainees. For the record, my male counterparts *did* have the 'Bible college' discussion early on. The thing I found most discouraging was this sense of a general lack of outcome. I was frustrated at the inability to progress within the Church unless I took an administrator role. I did the MAS with others; there was one guy who was doing well in the job. He had an opportunity to preach, and they changed him to a MiT (minister-in-training). I felt a bit like, 'Oh, even if I do well in this role, there is nothing that they can or will "promote" me to. But the guys have a clear path that they can work through.'

Rachel did everything right – but her gifts and calling couldn't be effectively channelled. Her service and apprenticeship, practically speaking, led nowhere.

Leak 2 No place to use certain gifts in the Church

Many friends of mine serve and flourish in their local church; many of them serve where there is need and serve joyfully. But some of them, despite being trained and equipped, have limited or no opportunity to use 'some' of the gifts that the Spirit has given them. Interestingly, these are often related to word or leadership gifts. Here is a story:

Lucy

I loved doing seminary; it challenged me to love God and read books I would never have read. I loved studying beside men passionate about building God's kingdom. I both rejoiced and struggled that many of these young men would go on to lead churches. Many would go on to be stretched and encouraged to do so. While at seminary, I had the opportunity to prepare preaching. But I had little opportunity to use this gift, apart from in evangelistic talks or at youth camp. It felt that, if I ever expressed a desire to use this gift, people would view this in a wrong way. That others would view me as clambering for power and platform, rather than seeking to glorify God. What was an honourable desire for men was not for me. During my third year, our study of church polity led me to ask questions about decisions in the Church. I began to understand that my frustrations came from the church structure. A structure that lacked accountability, transparency and a plurality of elders. Instead of equipping the whole body, many men and women were unable to thrive and grow and serve. I now attend a church where I too am stretched and encouraged in my giftings.

A lack of theological clarity can lead women such as Lucy to be unaware of what they can or can't do in the Church, and this often means that women don't serve with these gifts in church. Don't read that too quickly. Women represent half of the image of God; that's half of God's ambassadors potentially unsure and unclear about the role of women in the Church. I speak with pastors often: they are supportive but don't articulate their position. Lucy is a gifted communicator and theologian – and that is a gift that some churches have missed out on, because of a lack of clarity over how women can use these gifts.

Leak 3 Time pressures

Analysis from the Office for National Statistics has shown that women carry out an overall average of 60% more unpaid work than men. This is for cooking, childcare and housework.[3] Women genuinely seem to have more to juggle, with a variety of

---

3 Office for National Statistics, 'Women Shoulder the Responsibility of "Unpaid work"', Office for National Statistics, 10 November 2016: https://www.ons.gov.uk/employmentandlabourmarket/peopleinwork/earningsandworkinghours/articles/womenshouldertheresponsibilityofunpaidwork/2016-11-10 (accessed 14 September 2023).

responsibilities at different stages of life. All of this means that we need to be even more flexible when it comes to helping women flourish in church. Here are some stories of time pressures:

Eloise
An ex-women's worker once commented about the anti-social hours which make it very hard. To do her job she needs to work evenings. The women in her congregation are only free in the evening, not the daytime. But somehow she's expected to be in the office all day.

Mary
As a single woman in the Church, others often comment that I have more free time than most and that I should give it more to serve others in the Church.

Susie
I took time out of paid ministry to have children. There are so many time pressures on me. In general, mothers are more likely to flex their job around childcare. I have a friend whose husband is called to full-time ministry and so location and funds don't allow both to do this. Some women prioritise their husband's secular job. Others sacrificially care for ageing parents.

Susie, Mary and Eloise's experience should confront us with an interesting question: what are our church timetables based around? Beyond Sunday, are we assuming an old model where women are married and the wife is 'at home with the kids', and men work from 9 to 5 p.m.? Raising this question – that of time pressure – shows how this goes beyond gender to challenge our assumptions about class, type of work, shift patterns and parenting. What if thinking about enabling women to serve in our churches also ultimately released more men to serve too?

Leak 4 Inaccessibility and affordability of formal training

I'm intrigued as to why some churches pay for and send men to theological college but not women. This means that women must pay for themselves. I have two friends who are finishing working for the same charity. The man is being paid to pursue theological study alongside working part time for his church. The woman must raise her entire finances for fees, accommodation and cost of living and pay for herself to go. Both competent and gifted, yet the outcome and expectations are so different. Here is Lucy's story:

> Lucy
>
> I have always loved studying the Bible. When my youngest started school, I applied for a three-year course, but it was so expensive. The day the deposit had to be paid, I sat and wept and prayed with my kids because I didn't have a penny towards it. Most people taking the course would have their fees paid by the Church. But as a stay-at-home mum in that season, I didn't fit the usual criteria. I poured out my frustrations to God – it didn't seem fair that only rich people or boys got to go to seminary. God enabled me to leave it in his hands. And by the end of the day, God had not only provided the deposit but all the fees for Year 1 and half of Year 2 as well. It was incredible. I was the only woman on the whole course that year. But with six brothers, I was not uncomfortable around men, even if they (sometimes) were uncomfortable around me! Before we even started the course, I received an email from a fellow student asking me about travel arrangements to our first residential. As the only female in the email group, he had assumed I was the new administrator.

Lucy has shared a startling story of God's provision – but wrapped up in that is the assumption that she's partly there to facilitate travel arrangements! What could you do in your context to enable more women to grow theologically?

Leak 5 Lack of paid roles at appropriate levels

For many, once they experience 'time out' of paid work, for whatever reason, they find there is no job to which to return. In a longer story, Amy shares what this feels like:

Amy
Life in my mid twenties
It all seemed so simple in my mid twenties. The world was my oyster! I had done two years of a ministry apprentice scheme, spent two years abroad doing student ministry and three in the UK. I loved it and lapped up all the training I could get. I appreciated the training I received, and I could see myself, ten or fifteen years down the line, passing on what I had learnt. I could imagine speaking at training courses, supervising staff or writing training material.

When the student job came to an end, there was nothing obvious for me to move on to. I did apply for a student-worker job in a church, but nothing came of it. It seemed that the break from a full-time job came at a good time, because my husband and I were ready to start a family. Over the course of the next seven or so years, there wasn't much time to think about what I was going to move on to next. I was trying to be present with my kids and enjoy every moment. I do not have any regrets about this; I have loved being a mum. It's the best way I have ever spent my time and I would not change how I spent those years for anything. But when our youngest was due to start full-time school I started to wonder what was next for me. I asked myself whether there was a way back to ministry.
Life in my mid thirties
I was full of optimism at the start. It felt so exciting to think

83

of all the time I would have and I was hopeful of all the ways I could serve. I was grateful for the wealth of experience that I had gained over those years at home with my kids. I started to talk to folk in my church, who were nothing but supportive. The suggestion came up about doing some further training. There was even talk about there being a training budget which people in my position could make use of. I needed to make a plan, find a training course, something to study and a long-term aim. And finally, I needed to bring my idea to the church leaders.

This is where things started to unravel. I thought that the best route back into ministry was to do some sort of training course. But there didn't seem to be much out there for people in my position who wanted a way back into ministry after a break. Travelling or time away wasn't going to be possible for me with family life. Some of the shorter, more introductory courses were more possible, but felt like a step back. I could have bought course materials and tried to study something by myself. But that felt too demoralising and isolating.

Trying to find my way back

I didn't know where to take things from there. I knew that there would always be something to learn and enjoy if I did an introductory course. I didn't want to be proud, but when someone suggested I do the course that I had already done sixteen years previously, I was reeling. Hadn't I progressed since then? Was all my training and experience to that point worth nothing? Had it somehow expired, so that I needed to start all over again? I had imagined that I would be teaching on courses like this by the time I was 37. Rather, I was invited to take the course again because there was nothing else for me to move on to! What had gone wrong?

I am sure that, if I were driven enough, I could carve out a path for myself in this new phase of life. But I am not sure that is me, and it doesn't seem fair that that's the only way to make it in ministry as a woman. It all makes me wonder if it is worth it, and if my gifts, skills and experience would be better used elsewhere.

To be honest, I am enjoying using this extra time when my kids are at school in a variety of ways. All these ways are worthwhile and valuable – and maybe a full-time ministry job wouldn't suit me now. But I don't want to give up on the idea just because there is no well-worn path to follow. And I am curious – what has happened to all the women who started out on this training path sixteen years ago? Would many of them also have loved to return to a ministry job after their kids started school? Did any of them find their way back?

When I left college and started in student work it felt as if it was one of my only options for ministry. I wasn't interested in youth work (there are plenty of paid youth and children's worker roles around!). For the guys, it felt as if there was a pathway laid out for them: church intern, theological training, curacy/assistant pastor. But for women (especially those of us who are complementarian in our theology), you must work so hard to carve out your own path and you are lucky to get a post.

I'm sure this problem is more widespread than just women, or just student workers. So, let's pause and think about the wider situation of gifting within the Church.

Can we fix the leaky pipe?

To address the leaky pipe in the STEM world, scientists started assembling more data on gender bias, but here they hit a wall. Studies suggest that male STEM faculties evaluate research that demonstrates gender bias as significantly lower in quality than female STEM faculties do. I think we have a similar problem in the Church, and not just from men.

How we view each other matters. Key to fixing the leaky pipe is rediscovering truths found in Galatians 3. Truths that show why and how we relate to one another, not with suspicion but as co-heirs. The New Testament is brimming with examples of men and women working together, yet influences over history have led to a slippery slope where the ministry of women is far more restricted than in the Bible itself.

We come back to the issue of the three ghosts that haunt women in the church: the child, the temptress and the usurper. When women are seen like children, they are belittled and reduced to people to order around. When women are seen as temptresses, then it could seem inappropriate to mentor someone from the opposite sex. When women are seen as usurpers, we tend to be afraid and keep away, wary of losing our power. Our hesitation to work together is our biggest hindrance. We need one another; we need to function as a body.

Andrew Bartlett says:

> The traditional majority Christian view was robustly patriarchal. Women were inferior to men, both in rank and in nature. Men were the leaders in all spheres of life. As compared with men, women were regarded as inherently defective, being less intelligent, more prone to sin and unfit for the kinds of leadership which men were able to provide. They were not in God's image in the same full sense as men.[4]

The contrast between Jesus' view of women and that of the culture into which he was born has been a theme in this book, and it is vital to appreciate it. Into this context and against tradition, Jesus was radically different. Galatians 3 gives us our motivation:

---

4 Andrew Bartlett, *Men and Women in Christ: Fresh light from the biblical texts* (London: IVP, 2019), p. 38.

Now that this faith has come, we are no longer under a guardian.

So in Christ Jesus you are all children of God through faith, for all of you who were baptized into Christ have clothed yourselves with Christ. There is neither Jew nor Gentile, neither slave nor free, nor is there male and female, for you are all one in Christ Jesus. If you belong to Christ, you are Abraham's seed, and heirs according to the promise. (Galatians 3:25–29)

Here we see the unity and equal standing shared by all Christian believers. Because of Jesus, women are no longer treated as second-class citizens. Instead they are seen as sons and as sons they are heirs, they have full status and full rights of inheritance. With men, they are equal co-heirs of God's promise. This New Testament picture of women and men stands in stark contrast to the traditional majority view. The traditional majority view influenced how the early Church saw relationships between the two sexes. Let's consider some snapshots from the New Testament showing how men and women relate to one another in various ways in the life of the early Church.

Mentoring, supporting, sponsoring and leaning on one another across genders is biblical

- *Women to men*. Priscilla, Aquilla and Apollos in Acts 18. Priscilla and her husband taught Apollos, one of the chief teachers of the Church. This isn't new or shocking for most readers today. Yet the placing of her name for first-century readers would have been highly unusual. Priscilla was named first because she was probably the more intelligent and devoted of the two.

- *Women to women*. Naomi and Ruth in Ruth 1. Ruth risks everything in her commitment to her mother-in-law.
- *Men to women in groups*. Jesus and Mary in Luke 10. Against tradition, Mary sat with men and they learned together when custom would have had her serving with her sister Martha.
- *Men and women as co-workers*. Romans 16 is bursting with examples of women and men as co-workers. Men and women, brothers, sisters, mothers all working hard together. They were commended for their service; they were outstanding among the apostles and risked their lives together.
- *Men to women on their own*. Jesus and the Samaritan woman in John 4. Jesus discussed theology with a questionable woman.
- *Women as patrons*. Phoebe in Romans 16 was a wealthy influential person of high standing, providing substantial benefits to many believers, including Paul.
- *Grandmothers and mothers teaching men*. Timothy in 2 Timothy was taught by his mum Eunice and granny Lois.
- *Jesus and the apostles depending on women*. Only women are said to give general, regular financial provision (out of their own means) to Jesus and the Twelve in Luke 8:3.
- *Men and women travelling together*. Jesus allowed women who weren't his relatives to travel with him in his group of male and female disciples in Luke 8:1–3.
- *Women hosting assemblies of believers in their home*. Nympha in Colossians 4:15 provided hospitality and leadership for the house church in her home.
- *Men and women as brothers and sisters*. Paul instructs Timothy in 1 Timothy 5:1–2 and says, 'Treat younger men as brothers, older women as mothers, and younger women as sisters, with absolute purity.'

What do Rachel, Lucy, Eloise, Mary, Susie and Amy need to grow and flourish in serving the Church? They need men and women to recapture the heart of Galatians 3 as we interact and relate to one another as co-heirs. As my friend Elliot said to me in response to a difficult discussion about men and women: 'You are a gift to the Church and an heir of God himself.'

Questions for discussion

- Where do you identify yourself on the pipeline in Figure 3?
- Out of the above examples of how men and women relate in the New Testament, which surprises you the most?
- Where is the pipe leaking in your own church/network/charity? What would help you to plug the gaps in the pipeline?

Conclusion

I was travelling home from a conference and feeling overwhelmed. There had been very few women involved in a leadership or speaking role that week. Women were in the minority, and men and women were discouraged from mixing. I came away sad, disheartened and questioning the role of women in God's mission in our continent. I'd read the website and asked what their position was on women, but the response was, 'We don't have a position.'

The problem is that 'We don't have a position on the role of women in ministry' is not neutral. When you choose not to take an explicit position on the role of women in the Church, it leads to an implicit position. Clarity and consistency are essential, kind and biblical.

I was on the train home and revisited my favourite blog ('21 Places Women Emerge Front and Center in Scripture's Storyline') by Eric Schumacher.[1] I revisited Jesus' interactions with women and wept. I wept because what I read in Scripture felt so different from my experience that week. I wept because of the implications. I wept because the way that belief and practice drift further apart is so real. Yet, through my tears, I was reminded how much Jesus loved women. I saw again that he brought worth and value by healing, forgiving and restoring women. I saw again that he wasn't afraid to be in their company. He travelled in groups with women, he spoke to them on his own and even touched them. I saw again that he valued women's minds; he discussed theology with them and

---

1 Eric Schumacher, '21 Places Women Emerge Front and Center in Scripture's Storyline', The Gospel Coalition, 2 June 2018: https://www.thegospelcoalition.org/article/21-places-women-emerge-front-and-center-in-scriptures-storyline (accessed 13 September 2023).

included them when he taught. I saw again that he gave women a voice; he created opportunities for them to speak. Not only of their testimony. He asked them to speak about key essential truths of his birth, his identity and the resurrection. I sighed. I'd stopped crying and now was the time to live again.

In conclusion, I can identify three tensions. The first one is that, despite the goldmine of women gifted and equipped, they are short on support, opportunities and courage. Then there is the watching world that needs convincing about our message. Many believe that the Church and the Bible are misogynistic and sexist. Finally, there are leaders who want to encourage women to flourish in church, but are unsure how.

Tension 1 – gifted but held back

I've worked for so many years with excellent women. Repeatedly, I noticed that, after the initial five or so years of working, women seemed to disappear, although they were trained and equipped to as high a standard as the men. The men, on the other hand, kept working and often became pastors. I know some will say that not all men should be shoehorned into being a pastor, but at least it's something. As for the women, some needed time out for childcare and others didn't, but either way there was simply nothing for them; many women retired forty years early and gave up serving in that capacity. And it wasn't just these women: as I developed Passion for Evangelism, I met and engaged with many women, skilled and gifted yet unable to utilise some of their strongest gifting in their local church. There are waves and waves of these women and I'm convinced that, with a little investigation, you'll find them in your church.

But it's not just opportunities that women lack. Many struggle with confidence, failure and a fear of speaking out. Women struggle with the way they are viewed in the Church; they struggle with a lack of clarity and purpose. This then in turn has an impact on the core sibling relationship that is necessary for the Church to function as a body.

From my own experience, there are some deep-seated beliefs that hold women back. We need a conviction of calling that smashes the myth that gifted people are headhunted. We need a Spirit-inspired fearlessness that lessens the power of the myth of perfectionism. We need to be abounding in grace as we learn to trust that we are best placed; that even if someone else could do it better, we are uniquely called into our homes, workplaces, churches and communities.

Tension 2 – convinced that Christianity is oppressive

As men and women grow up in a feminist environment, many will be put off by churches and their overly restrictive views of women. Over and over again, I've heard of young women saying that there is no place for them in the Church. Women with teenage daughters have joined our book clubs, just to help their daughters see afresh what Jesus thinks of women. My friend told me about a conference for women and teenagers. Her friend came along with her 16-year-old daughter. She watched the speaker do a Bible overview and her jaw dropped. She said, 'Mum, I've never seen a woman teach the Bible before in any setting, let alone at a conference. I didn't know women could understand the Bible and share it with others.' Another friend said,

> I originally joined your PfE Book Club and bought this book because my teenage daughter struggles with women's roles within the Church. I think I've become quite accepting of it but would like to have a concise explanation when discussing it with her.

Our children and grandchildren are growing up in a feminist world, where their expectations of what women can do is radically different from those of previous generations. I recently went to pick up my car from the garage and the owner refused to let me drive out of the car park. Why was this? The last two women he had allowed to drive out crashed their cars. Me being me, I took the keys and attempted to run him over while shouting, 'Some women can drive, you know.' I told my eldest daughter and her eyes widened: 'But, Mum, that was so rude of him.' Like the mother above, many of us have come to be quite accepting of some of the everyday sexism that we see. However, a younger generation just won't stand for it. It's into this that we have an opportunity to speak clearly of Jesus' love for women.

Many men and women view Christianity through the lens of oppression rather than that of life-giving liberation. We need men and women to work together to point the watching world to a better story. As women and men proclaim the gospel together, we have an opportunity to show the world what restored, sibling relationships look like. Men and women working together in evangelism adorns the gospel! Women have opportunities to share the gospel in places and relationships in which men can't be involved. But if we limit who serves in church or in evangelism, I'm afraid this will turn some people off wanting to know more.

Tension 3 – keen but clueless

Throughout this book, I've identified some key issues for women as they seek to use their gifts to build up the local church alongside men. Pastors have written and asked for advice, and mostly I've said, 'Just talk to one another and listen.' Helping women to flourish is not as simple as just giving them opportunities. One male friend wrote to me and said, 'I can't believe it! I invited a woman to speak at our conference on evangelism and she said no, she'd rather sit in the audience and learn than be a speaker.' He continued, 'I'm trying, Nay!' I said to him, 'Go back to her, explain why you want her, why she is competent to do this and how you really think it would be great for the conference if she could.' He did and she said yes.

With encouragement, sponsorship and mentoring, there are so many doors that could be opened for women to contribute to and help build up the Church. I think of my friend Kenny who speaks at university missions. He wrote to me and said, 'I want to do this alongside women; could you suggest anyone?' Or Ed, who runs a podcast, wrote, asking, 'I want to give women an opportunity to speak evangelistically; could you suggest anyone?' Or Tom, who wrote, 'We're freeing up space on our blog and we'd love to feature more female authors.' Many of us, over the course of a week or year, will have opportunities where we can draw others alongside us: not just people who are like us, but who represent the diversity of the Church.

But, most of all, we need to learn to work together. I am so grateful for the five men in my life who have stood with me and journeyed with me. Turn back to the first couple of pages of this book and read the words of one of them, Dave Bish, as he shares his reflections on this book and on how we can move forwards.

Women matter to Jesus; you matter to Jesus. Would you join me and others in doing all we can to see, hear and honour women better?

Further reading

Introduction

Every year, more than 50% of people make New Year's resolutions, and that often includes a resolution to read more books. Yet almost every study tells us that around 80% of these resolutions will be abandoned by February. For some of us, reading is hard. Many of us will have started a new Bible reading plan or enthusiastically added to our 'to be read' list of books. For others, we'll have downloaded even more titles to listen to on Audible while enjoying a walk.

We know that reading books helps us to grow as disciples. We are convinced that the word of God is sweet to the taste, sweeter than honey. And yet it is so easy to move from high ambition to failure and relapse within the space of a few weeks. For many of us, that honey jar is just too far out of reach. According to World Book Day statistics, 41% of people in the UK spend less than an hour a week reading. So how do we read more and grow in knowledge and wisdom?

How and why we read matters. The character of C. S. Lewis in William Nicholson's play, *Shadowlands*, says, 'We read to know we are not alone.' We can see this is true in book sales throughout the pandemic. The 2021 bestsellers list shows book buyers seeking out comfort, laughter, escapism, familiarity and a sense of community. I'd encourage you, if you are feeling alone in the topics that have been raised in this book, to start reading. But don't do it on your own. Many of these books I've read in our PfE Book Clubs. We have women of all ages and church backgrounds discussing books from across the world. Here are some of the books I've read over the last few years as I've engaged with this topic of what women need to flourish in the Church.

Three must reads

Worthy: Celebrating the value of women by Elyse Fitzpatrick
and Eric Schumacher. This is probably the single most helpful
book I've ever read on the value of women in the Bible. It's a
must read for anyone who is struggling with what they think
Christianity says about women. Here is a condensed version
which inspired Eric and Elyse to write more: https://www.
thegospelcoalition.org/article/21-places-women-emerge-front-
and-center-in-scriptures-storyline.

*Developing Female Leaders: Navigate the minefields and release
the potential of women* by Kadi Cole. This book is based on
a US multi-site church experience. There is much within this
book that you can apply to your own setting. It focuses on the
unique issues of raising female leaders and provides lots of
practical help based on the experience and wisdom of working
with many church leaders.

Why Can't We Be Friends? Avoidance is not purity by Aimee
Byrd. This is a key book that is the backbone of the vision for
men and women working together as co-workers, disciples and
siblings.

More books to read

1 Understanding our culture

This whole section has really helped me to understand some of the
contentions of bias against women in society.

*The Confidence Code: The science and art of self-assurance:
What women should know* by Claire Shipman and Katty Kay.
If we could find the key or the code to confidence, then surely
we could just apply that to women who need it? This book helps

to identify a confidence problem in women across the world. As one friend said, 'Nay loves a depressing story.' But for me, this book was what kickstarted my thinking into observing more closely what was happening in churches. It also helped to validate some of the things I had been thinking about myself.

The Authority Gap: Why women are still taken less seriously than men, and what we can do about it by Mary Ann Sieghart. This book looks at many situations where there is a difference in the way people are treated in their society, according to their gender. It is so helpful for establishing the context, and understanding the wider society, in which women are growing up.

Invisible Women: Exposing the gender bias women face every day by Caroline Criado Perez. This book looks at statistical evidence for gender bias. One of the important elements of change is stopping, observing and identifying the problems. This book was a very clear example of how to do this by listening to women's stories and pursuing change.

2 Getting to know the women of the Bible

Phoebe: A story by Paula Gooder. I took this on a summer holiday and couldn't put it down. Is there a place for a Phoebe in our Church today? It's easy to get into a rut about what we think women can and can't do. However, reading stories of women from the Bible, such as this, reminds us that God sees women as crucial and indispensable to his mission.

Lost Women of the Bible: The women we thought we knew by Carolyn Custis James. Carolyn introduces you to women from the Bible and retells their stories. As the title suggests, we think we know these women, but often we don't. I found this book, particularly the chapter on Hagar, very helpful. The author talks about the invisibility of Hagar to society, but describes her as a woman who is seen by God.

Women and Work in the Old Testament by Theology of Work Project, The Bible and Your Work Study Series. I read this years ago and it blew my mind. It's a short Bible study series on women from the Old Testament with a particular focus on application in the workplace. I was particularly struck by the boldness and courage of the midwives in Genesis standing up to a ruler who was insisting on genocide of male babies.

Forty Women: Unseen women of the Bible from Eden to Easter by Ros Clarke. Ros doesn't hold back in the way she retells the stories of these women. At points, it feels explosive and shows that the Bible doesn't shy away from some of the toughest subjects that women face.

Jesus through the Eyes of Women: How the first female disciples help us know and love the Lord by Rebecca McLaughlin. This is an excellent book that looks at Jesus afresh through the women he met, taking you through different themes. I found it very hard to finish as I kept pausing throughout. It felt timely and deeply profound.

3 Apologetics

What Is a Girl Worth? My story of breaking the silence and exposing the truth about Larry Nassar and USA gymnastics by Rachael Denhollander. This is such a sad, true story of abuse in US gymnastics. It's a tale of whistleblowing and fighting for justice and truth, which is well told and points to hope throughout.

Confronting Christianity: 12 hard questions for the world's largest religion by Rebecca McLaughlin. Increasingly, friends and friends' daughters are commenting about whether their church's stance on women leads them to question whether they have a place in the Church. This book addresses the huge question of whether God is anti-women.

4 Looking at the issues women face in the Church

'3 Female Ghosts That Haunt the Church' by Jen Wilkin. This
excellent blog post summarises how some women can be
treated in the Church. Many women, after reading this, have
identified with it. Reading this alongside other books in this
list will show you the stark contrast between Jesus' treatment of
women and the Church's.

*Recovering from Biblical Manhood & Womanhood: How the
Church needs to rediscover her purpose* by Aimee Byrd.
This book is a response to *Recovering Biblical Manhood &
Womanhood* edited by Wayne Grudem and John Piper. The
original and Aimee's book are important to read, in order
to hear what is being said. So many now see that theological
viewpoints on women can be horrendously misapplied. It's only
by listening carefully, rather than presuming, that we begin to
see the glaring blind spots.

Liberated: How the Bible exalts and dignifies women by Karen
Soole. Covering themes relevant to women in society today,
Karen gives an overview of the Bible, addressing the essential
topic of how the Bible treats women. This is an excellent book
to read and discuss with friends.

Gospel Women: Studies of the named women in the Gospels by
Richard Bauckham. Rather than offering a general overview
of the Gospel women or focusing on a single theme, Richard
Bauckham studies in great depth both the individual women
who appear in the Gospels and the specific passages in which
they appear. I found the chapters on the naming of women very
significant. This book also added depth to my understanding of
the social context of women in the New Testament.

Men and Women in Christ: Fresh light from the biblical texts
by Andrew Bartlett. There are so many books defending one
position or attacking another. Andrew looks afresh at the
passages from his background as a judge and arbitrator. He uses

fresh language and asks questions that make you investigate familiar passages again. For anyone struggling to know where they fit in or what to believe in the debate about women's roles in the Church, this is an excellent place to go.

Paul and Gender: Reclaiming the Apostle's vision for men and women in Christ by Cynthia L. Westfall. A respected New Testament scholar offers a coherent Pauline theology of gender, which includes fresh perspectives on the most controversial texts.

5 Women in mission

Women in God's Mission: Accepting the invitation to serve and lead by Mary T. Lederleitner. This book looks at anecdotal stories of women in mission across the world. Mary's definition of mission is quite broad, but many have found this a helpful read as it looks at some of the issues that women face, showing how they have continued to build up the Church, despite difficulties. I read this with a small group of women from across Europe, some of whom had gifting they couldn't use in the Church. This book encouraged them to pioneer and seek opportunities where they couldn't yet see them.

Not Less Than Everything: The courageous women who carried the Christian gospel to China by Valerie Griffiths. This is a detailed history of women who took the gospel to China in the 1800s and 1900s. It includes stories of the Chinese Bible women who did the incredible work of sharing the gospel stories with women in China.